Alpe d'Huez
the legend

Tour de France, L'Alpe d'Huez le légende

© 2003 Cabal Communications Ltd

Alpe d'Huez : The Legend
© 2003 VeloPress, American edition

Printed in France

10 9 8 7 6 5 4 3 2 1

Distributed in the United States and Canada by Publishers Group West.

International Standard Book Number : 1-931382-37-9

Library of Congress Cataloging-in-Publication Data applied for.

VeloPress
1830 North 55th Street
Boulder, Colorado 80301–2700 USA
303/440-0601; Fax 303/444-6788;
Email velopress@7dogs.com

To purchase additional copies of this book or other VeloPress books, call 800/234-8356 or visit us on the Web at velopress.com.

A book by Gérard Ejnès

With Philippe Bouvet, Raoul Dufourcq et Serge Laget, and journalists, reports, articles and photographs from L'Équipe

Design : Bernard Fournier and Jacques Hennaux
Reproduction : Rampazzo & Associés
Iconographie : Philippe Le Men et Christian Naitslimane

English language version
Translation : Ellis Bacon, Peter Cossins, Duncan Steer
Design : Julie Hewett

Alpe d'Huez the legend

Foreword

Twenty-three visits to the Alpe and 100 years of the Tour de France. This is a unique event, a monumental occasion. A true meeting of giants. On July 13, 2003 while the Tour is joyously celebrating its centenary, the ski station at Alpe d'Huez will be welcoming 'la Grande Boucle' for the 23rd time.

On this great occasion I'd like to pay tribute to my predecessors from the Oisans area and particularly to Georges Rajon. I would like to send my thanks to all those who have shown their faith in this association with the Tour de France and who have made the Alpe d'Huez stage of the Tour de France such a prestigious event, and one that arouses such feelings of expectation. Thanks to them and also to the organisers of the Tour de France, Jacques Goddet, Félix Lévitan and, more recently, Jean-Marie Leblanc, this climb has taken on a mythical aspect. For the Dutch who have won here so often, as you will soon discover as read this book produced in partnership with L'Equipe, it has become even more important than the world championship!

To celebrate this special anniversary, the municipality is bringing together all of the riders who have won on Alpe d'Huez, and a trophy engraved with all of their names will be unveiled in their presence.

But we wanted to do something even beyond this, hence the publication of this book for all fans of cycling, whether French or from abroad. For them this book will be a beautiful souvenir of an incomparable mountain. Quite simply, this is 'the legend of Alpe d'Huez'.

I'd like to offer many thanks to the Tour de France for its contribution in building the huge notoriety of this special place, and also send thanks to all those who have helped to make this stage such a success for our region.

Long live the Tour de France and happy birthday

ERIC MULLER
THE MAYOR OF ALPE D'HUEZ

Preface

The Alpe! It's like all the Alps encapsulated in one moun- tain. It offers an evocative and impressive résumé of so many mountain adventures. And its 21 bends are packed with so many great stories, the kind of myths that are the foundation of the Tour de France, now in its hundredth year. There is no doubt that Alpe d'Huez plays an important part in the Tour's history, even though it was only visited for the first time scarcely more than 50 years ago, when Fausto Coppi, the Campionissimo, hauled its bird-like countenance up to the first ever summit finish in Tour history. Even back then in 1952, the Tour was already beginning to spin its web of sporting history. However, we had to wait almost 25 years, until 1976, when the links between the mountain and the Tour were re-established and the marriage between them was cemented.

From that point on, that magical mountain became one of the greatest natural stadiums in the world. Hundreds of thousands of spectators rub shoulders there on a given day in July, creating a noisy, clamouring mass of humanity urging on with shouts, flags and gestures every rider that passes them on this most testing of roads. It's a love story written with the sweat of champions and of their enthusiastic fans, and we will be telling you about both in this book. You'll see that what was once the mountain of the Dutch - with eight victories between 1976 and 1989 - has developed an international flavour in recent seasons, notably with the victory of Lance Armstrong in 2001, a champion who seems to come from a different world.

And watching all the action since 1952 has been the newspaper L'Equipe, whose pages are reproduced in this book to emphasise the greatness of the feats achieved here. Among them are the pages recalling the victory of Bernard Hinault, the only French winner in this mythical place, in 1986 at the end of a stage that produced the perfect mix of sporting spectacle and human spirit. As well as the pages from L'Equipe, we also hope you enjoy the newpaper's pictures that offer a gripping momento of the joy and suffering that has been seen on the Alpe, plus extracts from the past from some of L'Equipe's most renowned writers and contributors.

L'Equipe and the municipality of Alpe d'Huez are proud to bring you the history of this unique place.

GÉRARD EJNÈS
ASSISTANT EDITORIAL DIRECTOR OF L'EQUIPE

TWENTY-ONE STEPS TO CYCLING MYTHOLOGY

The Alpe and its 21 hairpins have been transformed into the ultimate high point of the Tour. It's a place where the unworthy are found out, because they will last maybe three hairpins before the truth hits them... This is why the result the Alpe produces is always the right one. Pellos, the master of cycling cartoonists, said this climb reminded him of his cartoons from the 1930s of mountains standing in judgement over cyclists... There is no way to cheat this mountain...

Alpe d'Huez always produces the same feeling of anticipation. The first impression is of the array of colours produced by the massed ranks in front of the stunning backdrop of the Oisans mountain scenery. The noise begins to build on the climb out of Bourg and swells on the way through each of the 21 most famous hairpins on the route of the Tour de France. On the day the Tour visits the mountain, it is like a huge beehive buzzing frantically with activity and noise.

Passing through Bourg d'Oisans, right in the shadow of the mythical mountain, even the greatest of champions can be humbled by the occasion and setting, especially if the day has been a long one and the race has already passed over the Croix de Fer, the Galibier or the Glandon. The initial slopes of the Alpe demand a brutal change of rhythm and every ounce of effort. Every rider, from the yellow jersey to the last man, is almost carried along by the frenzy that surrounds them and that gives some sense to the suffering they are enduring. The church tower in Oisans is the first landmark, marking the first section of this staircase with no landing. It's best for the riders to keep their gaze set on their front wheel. If they were to raise their heads, even though they wouldn't dream of doing so, they would be able to make out the ski station still so far and so high up amongst the peaks...

The Tour de France has already been to this 'must-visit' place on 22 previous occasions, and it always offers an unmatchable welcome. There was no question that it had to be revisited during the centenary edition of the great adventure that is the Tour de France, a race sprinkled this year with its most famous summits. It was here at Alpe d'Huez that the first ever summit finish took place. Naturally, it was one of the sport's mythical figures, Fausto Coppi, who was the first winner on the Alpe in 1952, the year when the Campionissimo rode in a state of grace and simply outclassed his rivals.

The turning point for the climb was the 1970s and 1980s, an era when the world's press used to compose their stories in the ski station's church and when the mountain's priest was Dutch. A long line of climbers from that lowland country tasted success on the legendary peak: Zoetemelk, Kuiper and Winnen on no less than two occasions each; then Rooks and Theunisse. However, the rest of the world also featured: there was a Portuguese winner (Agostinho); a Swiss winner (Breu); a Colombian (Herrera); a Spaniard (Echave); two Americans (Hampsten and Armstrong); and Italians, lots of Italians (Coppi, Bugno, Conti, Pantani, Guerini); and thankfully there was also a French winner, Bernard Hinault, arguably the strongest of them all. He left a deep impression on the Alpe when he crossed the line hand in hand with his young team-mate, Greg LeMond, for whom he had played the role of the St Bernard guiding the lost soul to safety on the mountain. An American was to win the Tour for the first time, but on Alpe d'Huez Bernard Hinault had made a success of the most difficult role of all – that of bowing out of the sport.

Most of the legendary climbers have tasted success on the Alpe, almost as a point of honour: Luis Herrera, the Colombian with the spindly legs; and Marco Pantani, of course, who still holds the official record time for the climb – 37 minutes 35 seconds achieved in 1997 for the 14.5-kilometre-long climb. A setting of stupendous beauty, Alpe d'Huez, a stage of mythical exploits and dreadful failures, has often proved to be the real finale of the Tour. And now, as the Tour begins its second century of existence, let's commit ourselves to a promise: that the Alpe is revisited as often as possible.

PHILIPPE BOUVET

IT'S HARD TO MAKE OUT FROM SO FAR ABOVE, but on July 14, 1988, the Dutchmen Rooks and Theunisse, acclaimed by 50,000 of their compatriots, miraculously transformed the Alpe into a festival of orange.

THE ALPE IN 1988,
WHEN A CANADIAN
RIDER SHOULDERED
THE YELLOW
JERSEY. Climbing up
through these hairpins
Steve Bauer had his
yellow jersey pinched
by Pedro Delgado, who
went on to win in
Paris.

AS THE SCREENWRITER JOSÉ GIOVANNI ONCE
SAID, the hairpins of the Tour transform "the mountains
into a giant alphabet", and here we can make out the
'V', of 'Vive l'Alpe' perhaps.

THE GUT-CHURNING REPUTATION OF THE ALPE was much in evidence in 1988, when a much-thinned-down peloton struggles upwards after Bernard, Breukink, Kelly, Mottet and Hampsten have cracked.

NO, THE RIDERS HAVEN'T BEEN EATEN UP BY THE MYSTERIOUS YETI OF VERCOURS, because you can just make them out high up – there, on the right, pushing themselves towards the col.

THE RIDERS CURSE, gasp, groan, gasp again and suffer, while the holiday-makers encourage them, applaud them, acclaim them.

WHEN THE HAIRPINS start to look like the branches of the fir trees eulogised by the poet Guillaume Apollinaire is the precise moment when the riders start to curse quietly to themselves.

Emblematic...

The climb of Alpe d'Huez has become a race within a race, a spectacle apart from the rest of the Tour, a battleground that is totally unique.

THROUGH 89 EDITIONS AND 100 YEARS OF HISTORY AND EXPLOITS, the Tour has become encapsulated by its high points, from Sainte-Marie de Campan where Eugène Christophe reworked his broken forks in the forge, to the Puy-de-Dôme where Anquetil and Poulidor duelled through the heat and their exhaustion, to the Izoard where Bobet took flight, and the Galibier where Garrigou cut a route across the snowfields. However, none of these places, despite the epic deeds seen on them, the emotions they arouse and the legends attached to them, can match the magic nor the magnetism of the Alpe. To explain why this is so would be impossible, pretentious even. It would be like, for example, trying to explain the majesty of Macchu Picchu.

In order to say they have been there and to savour that atmosphere, fans climb the mountain on foot, in groups, with their families, they camp and take shelter on those slopes. Plotting all those individual journeys, right from Coppi's baptism of fire in 1952, would be an impossible task, but if you were to do so the final picture would be like a Bayeux tapestry of modern times. The picture would be like the crossing of the English Channel and the battle of Hastings repeated 22 times and multiplied by the 21 bends.

Each episode in the serial would reveal a vivid, noisy, colourful mass of humanity, generations of fans from every culture and speaking every language from all over the world and rubbing shoulders with each other, and each with their individual whims: "Vas-y Robic", "Allez le Blaireau", "Go on, Lance," and all kinds of other cries in Dutch, English, Italian, German...

The mountain becomes a living monument of noise and emotion, where thousands of motorhomes and 4x4s bring many more thousands of fans, who daub their imprecations on the tarmac, and watch the action unfold in front of them with fevered passion. On these 21 hairpins, just as they do on the 22 sectors of pavé at Paris-Roubaix, the spectators become part of the action and create the ambience. The race almost bounces off the fans from one hairpin to the next, tipped one way and then the other. Those 21 bends become a compressed version of the whole 21-day race. And you have to wonder if there was a tapestry reflecting events on the Alpe, how it would seem to people in 200 years' time who wanted to know more about life in the 20th and 21st centuries. Would it seem totally absurd to them?

SERGE LAGET

AS WELL AS THE RACING, the Alpe is also thousands of hands reaching to grab trinkets and gadgets from the caravan, applauding the riders, pushing them, and writing gigantic words of encouragement...

ONCE AGAIN THE MOUNTAIN GOES DUTCH. It's 1988 and Steven Rooks is heading for glory as stragglers struggle past the church in Oisans.

UP HERE,
EVERYTHING THAT
ISN'T BENT OVER IS
AT LEAST SLOPING –
the roofs, the trees, the
fans, and even the
riders. But they cling to
the winding road in
their quest for the
mythical place that lurks
just above them at the
finish.

THE RECIPE THAT HAS MADE THE ALPE so famous is captured in this moment – a great climber powering upwards in yellow, in this case Ullrich in 1997, with two cars, three motorbikes and dozens of rows of witnesses.

THERE'S NO NEED FOR A STATUE OF LIBERTY to signal that the suffering is over. Some modest tower blocks are all that are needed for agonised faces to lose some of their pain.

THE PINNACLE. The final straight, the rush felt as they finally arrive at the end. All the apparatus and pomp of the Tour is waiting, and there are still a few more steps, the last ones and the easiest of all, up onto the podium.

PERHAPS THE MOST STUNNING FINALE TO A TOUR stage was in 1986, when Greg LeMond and Bernard Hinault, after a heated exchange that made for great viewing, crossed the line with arms clasped in friendship.

1952: COPPI AND ROBIC PAVE THE WAY

In 1952 the snow was already attracting a lot of people to Alpe d'Huez, but the ski station's hoteliers were looking for an idea that would enable them to sell the resort out of season. It was an artist from Bourg d'Oisans, Jean Barbaglia, who was also a real fan of cycling, who had the idea of taking the Tour de France up to the summit. The idea was rewarded with an epic duel and the victory of a legendary champion.

It took Bianchi's great champion Fausto Coppi 45 minutes 22 seconds to climb the 14 kilometres that rise 1,080 metres at an average of 7.7%. In other words he climbed the mountain at an average of 18.664 kilometres per hour. He reached the foot of the climb with a number of other riders, but on it he thrashed them so comprehensively that all of them – apart from Jean Robic who rode as if possessed – came in more than three minutes behind Coppi. The gap between Coppi and the third man, Stan Ockers, was 3-22, or 7% longer than it took the Italian to scale the mountain. The 12th man to finish, Coppi's great rival Gino Bartali, was five minutes back and took no less than 12% longer. Excuse all the figures, but there are few better ways to express the magnificence of Fausto Coppi's exploit and to demonstrate how this one climb defined so clearly Coppi's huge talent and capacity in 1952. Athletics and swimming, two sports based fundamentally on the clock, have never known such large gaps. The third finisher in the Olympic 800-metre final would never finish more than seven seconds behind the winner (which would be the margin based on a 7% difference in their times), but on this unforgettable occasion the winner really produced something phenomenal. Fausto Coppi was a champion without measure.

Just a single rider had the ability to take on Coppi. More aggressive than ever, grimacing frighteningly, Robic had been known as 'Biquet' (the kid) for several years. It wasn't up to him to take up the challenge and increase the pace in the valley; instead he wisely sat in the wheels hoping to profit from the hard graft the riders from the Italian squadra were undertaking.

A man who liked being in the thick of the action, the little climber attacked the brutal initial slopes of the mountain with great fury in the company of Géminiani, who, although it was already too late for him to win the race, still wanted

JULY 6, 1952
Jean Robic has attacked first on the initial ramps of Alpe d'Huez on the way out of Bourg d'Oisans. Riding with great panache he will resist Fausto Coppi until six kilometres from the summit.

to show that he was prepared to attack. But this show of arms brought an immediate riposte from Coppi. Delayed for so long during the day, battle was now engaged.

The magisterial Italian champion, who had been directly provoked, would now show just what he was made of: he would get across to Robic. Quite quickly, it was clear that 'Gem' couldn't follow Robic's diabolical pace. As he fell back, Coppi came forwards stylishly, cutting the deficit on the Breton who had established a clear advantage over the first three kilometres. Behind them, considerable gaps were already appearing. Then Coppi, having got up to Robic, went to the front as was his custom, laying down his own pace, a pace that was relentless in its mechanical simplicity and style.

Robic hung on, and on, and on, but then... Almost as if he was unaware there was another rider with him, Fausto, without even turning to look, accelerated and then, somehow aware of the desperate resistance behind, accelerated yet again. That was it, the gap had been created: he went 25 metres clear almost immediately. There was still six kilometres to the summit. Coppi had flown. As he went around the corners, the Italian eagle shot a glance towards the distant valley below, urged on by his team manager Binda, who, very astutely, made his team leader well aware of the importance of the time gaps he could build on his rivals.

Behind the two heroes at the front of the race, there were any number of good performances, but they were forgotten due to what had gone before. Only later did it become obvious that Coppi's superlative performance would never be forgotten, but at the same time it should not mask the valour of those who were battling in his wake.

JACQUES GODDET
L'EQUIPE, JULY 6, 1952

Coppi is provoked into action

It was Robic who pushed Coppi into making an attack. But Coppi was also responding to the secret hopes of his directeur sportif.

"GO ON, FAUSTO, you'll soon see that he doesn't want to take the yellow jersey from you today." The Italian directeur sportif Alfredo Binda was right, and Coppi, sitting in a hot bath in his hotel that evening, didn't need to be coaxed into admitting as much. "I don't understand it all really! I left Lausanne this morning with the firm idea of staying on the defensive. But the French pushed me into responding after they had attacked. It was Robic initially, then Géminiani. I couldn't stay in the wheels any longer, and decided to play my own card. I didn't think I'd climb as well as that. But once I got up to Robic I grew in confidence. I pushed on twice to test him, then eased off. On the third occasion I gave it all I had in order to drop him. That Robic really is an incredible rider! I was expecting an attempt from Nello Laurédi to regain the yellow jersey today, but it was Robic who attacked. I think I'm going to have to watch out for him now."

Robic also admitted that he had had no intention of going on the attack at the start of the day. "It was only when we reached Bourg d'Oisans and I still felt good that I went on the offensive, while at the same time being careful not to upset Laurédi, who had told us he wanted to regain the jersey." Of course, Robic has good reason for saying this: he wouldn't want people to say that he neglected the leader of the French team.

ALBERT DE WETTER

L'EQUIPE, JULY 6, 1952.

IT'S ALMOST ALL OVER FOR ROBIC. Eight kilometres from the summit, Coppi steadily works his way back onto the Frenchman's wheel, his mind totally focused and without giving the impression that he's pushing himself hard at all. Coppi is simply astounding!

FOR A COUPLE OF KILOMETRES COPPI TESTS ROBIC OUT. He goes to the front and then ups the pace. Robic comes back to him. He tries a second time and Robic gets back on. But on the third occasion Coppi persists. Robic tries but can't stay with him. Without turning his head, as if all alone in the world, Coppi accelerates again and is gone.

MADAME ROBIC, no doubt a little disappointed, receives a kiss from her husband, a champion who fought bravely and with panache against a truly extraordinary champion. On that day at Alpe d'Huez, it was simply a case of Coppi and the rest. Robic has no reason for regrets.

THE DAY'S GREAT VICTOR is greeted at the finish by the French Secretary of State for Youth and Sports, Jean Masson (right), who followed the stage from beginning to end. On the right is Alfredo Binda.

AS WELL AS THE SUMMIT FINISH at the Alpe d'Huez ski station, the riders were rewarded with a rest day. In a relaxed mood, the two Italian champions Coppi and Bartali receive the press on the third floor of the Hotel Christina, and then take the opportunity to sign their lucrative post-Tour appearance contracts.

IN JULY, AT THE SKI STATION AS THE TOUR ARRIVES

"Alpe d'Huez is the only stage town where the press room is located in a church. Telex machines have taken over the sacristy and there are television screens under the organ. This house of God has rediscovered its original raison d'être: it's a cultural centre, a house of refuge, a place of sanctuary." In 1983, Jean Amadou was as inspired by the place as Antoine Blondin was five years earlier when writing the following article entitled "The Sundays of Life."

This title, borrowed from a famous painting by the Flemish artist Breughel, reflects the subject in hand. It's not really that extraordinary to spend an hour of your Sunday in church. It's rather more unusual, however, to find a church transformed into a press room of rather rustic proportions. Such was the case with the Notre-Dame-des-Neiges, in the parish of Alpe d'Huez, a building that is well worth a detour from the Tour. The exceptional architecture of this chalet-cathedral celebrates the marriage of concrete and wood. The robustness of the former combines with the natural grace of the latter and is reflected in the interior, a setting that is eminently inspiring. There is no better place to spend a day devoted to elevation, in all its forms. And as we sat in the stalls beavering away on our stories, we could have been mistaken for members of the clergy preparing our sermons.

By virtue of the fact that the house of God is a house to everyone, Notre-Dame-des-Neiges is open to all kinds of religions, the ecumenical on this occasion mixing with artistic or sporting beliefs. Perhaps yesterday's action did not totally fit in with the beliefs of the priest, but he organised for some younger members of the choir to celebrate the glory of Joop Zoetemelk and promised to ring the bells if the Dutchman proved successful. In the end, he didn't do too badly with his prediction of the result of the stage: his top three were Lubberding, Zoetemelk and Kuiper. But that's because the priest, Father Reuten, Jaap to those who know him well, is himself Dutch.

He came to the region 30 years ago, and what's more, was the representative in the Dauphiné area of a Dutch brand of beer, a position that enabled him to underwrite in part the construction of his masterpiece. "You are beer and on this beer I will build my church," you could perhaps say without causing too much offence.

The Sundays of life don't all seem the same to Joseph Bruyère, despite the fact that his patron saint looks down on the altar of the Notre-Dame-des-Neiges. Eight days ago he set out on a week-long cruise in yellow, and it seems he didn't get it at a reduced rate if the amount of energy he's expended in the intervening period is anything to go by. For him, the climb to Alpe d'Huez was like a descent into hell. He was burned to a crisp by the finish. Meanwhile, his compatriot and adversary Michel Pollentier had stirred his strangely-shaped body into action and had taken over the lead. The experts were saying that there must have been some kind of miracle... And there was a miracle in an unforeseen sense: Pollentier was thrown out of the race. The dragon with the bad habits had slain the archangel in this Michel. The shame was that if we'd had the news earlier, the priest could have rung the bells, because it's the Dutchman Zoetemelk who will be leaving his parish with the yellow jersey. But would it have been right to put out the flags when you've discovered there's a devil in the font?

ANTOINE BLONDIN
L'EQUIPE, JULY 17, 1978

IF SPORT IS A RELIGION, then the press room at Alpe d'Huez has long been its favoured sanctuary. In 1986, right under the organ, Greg LeMond and Bernard Hinault, flanking their directeur sportif Paul Koechli, reflect on the symphony they wrote the day before on the 21 climbs to the summit, before crossing the line hand in hand in a divine show of sharing.

BEFORE THE TOUR ARRIVES, it is already here. The 21 bends and a cortege of legends make their way across the giant screen at the summit.

THE TOUR DE FRANCE IS AN ENORMOUS MACHINE. When its infrastructure has been set down in a ski station like Alpe d'Huez, only the first step has been accomplished. Around the finish area preparations are made for transmission and retransmission of the action. The Tour de France will get the whole world talking about the action and the glory of the resort.

Time to rest and reflect

A rest day for the riders leaves the press jittery as they look for inspiration for the pages that still need to be filled.

THIS REST DAY HASN'T BEEN much like the ones we've experienced before. At this stage of the race in previous seasons, the race has been pretty much decided, and no one could really envisage there being much changing around of the positions already established. But this year anything can still happen. This Tour has not finished starting yet. An air of reflection is hanging over the race. Fignon must have been having some doubts even if Guimard was trying to persuade him not to. Guimard will have been looking at his man in the yellow jersey and seeing a man with a rather pale aspect.

The thoughts going through the riders' heads are nothing compared to the storms raging in the heads of the specialised cycling journalists – those people who have seen everything, analysed everything, and retained every fact. These men know the Tour de France as well as the French minister of finance knows their bank accounts. But all they know for the time being is who will not win the Tour. There is an air of humility beneath the snow on the white peak.

In the evening after spending the day taking part in a tennis tournament or playing boules, the press room started to buzz again. It's the time when the finish would be taking place on a normal day, and it's certainly true that the journalists begin to salivate like Pavlov's dogs at just this time of evening. I started my story on the terrace of the hotel, but inspiration wouldn't come. There were too many distractions: from the snowy summits down to the ladies passing by in their summer dresses, there were too many reasons for turning away from the blank page. In the end I went to the press room to finish the piece in amongst the clattering noise of my colleagues' typewriters. Some will think that inspiration didn't come, but my editor-in-chief, philosopher that he is, doesn't demand that my stories are inspired, only that they are delivered on time.

JEAN AMADOU
L'EQUIPE, JULY 19, 1983

Above from left to right:
REACHING THE FINISHING LINE is like arriving at the focal point of cycling's cathedral. On the Alpe, as elsewhere, joy and pain mix freely.

IT ALL STARTS after a very long wait. Cycling is nourished by both passion and patience. After the calm, the storm arrives.

AT THE END OF THE 21 BENDS entering into the ski station is a relief. As the riders pass under the kilometre banner (as the German Ullrich is about to here), the die has usually been cast.

THE TOUR DE FRANCE is also all about its sponsors. They are made to feel right at home on the Alpe. The chosen few won't miss anything at the finish of this epic stage.

THE OTHER SIDE OF THE PICTURE for the yellow jersey. In 1990, Ronan Pensec receives the most precious of rewards. He enjoys what is a rare moment in front of the crowd and the mountain he has tamed.

IN 1966, a Tour stage is to start in Bourg d'Oisans. Jacques Anquetil (right) and his team-mate Lucien Aimar, who will go on to win the race, are staying at Alpe d'Huez, where they mix with the French ski team who are preparing for the world championships in Portillo.

A CHANCE for Greg LeMond to relax with his family at the ski station in 1986. A few days later the American will take his first Tour de France win.

ON THE REST DAY IN 1978, Joop Zoetemelk reads about the incredible story of the disqualification of the Belgian Pollentier, which has made the Dutchman the surprised holder of the yellow jersey.

AS THE CHURCH has become too small, the resort's sports hall now hosts the ever-growing press pack who come to relate the story of the ascent through the 21 bends at Alpe d'Huez.

WHEN THE TOUR DE FRANCE decides to pass this way, the road to Alpe d'Huez becomes the world's biggest canvas. For several days, makeshift artists transform the road into a kaleidoscope of colour in order to sing the praises of their heroes and shout out tarmacadamed cries of praise. The riders climb up along an uninterrupted line of heartfelt devotions.

THE KINGDOM OF THE DUTCH

Between 1976 (Joop Zoetemelk) and 1989 (Gert-Jan Theunisse) Dutch riders took no less than eight wins at the summit of Alpe d'Huez. It became a real banker for them. The famous Dutch radio journalist Harrie Janssen said during this period: "For the sponsors, for the fans and for the riders, victory at Alpe d'Huez is more important than the world title."

At five o'clock in the afternoon on July 14, 1988, the bells of Notre-Dame-des-Neiges, in Alpe d'Huez, suddenly began to peal out. It wasn't to celebrate the taking of the Bastille, but was actually the church's priest, Father Jaap Reuten, a Dutchman, celebrating the one-two finish produced by compatriots Steven Rooks, from the nice little town of Otterleck, and Gert-Jan Theunisse, who hails from Oss, in one of the most prestigious stages of the Tour de France, which had finished at the top of the steep slopes leading to the Dauphiné ski station. This has become the normal state of affairs since Joop Zoetemelk was triumphant here in 1976, and since when the Dutch have insisted that their riders plant their tricolour blue, white and red flag on the summit.

After two wins by Kuiper – the second helped by Fate in the shape of Pollentier's disqualification after he tried to pull the wool over the officials' eyes at the doping control – then two by Zoetemelk, then Winnen taking another two, almost as if the Dutch, like policemen, only come along in twos, yesterday there was another beautiful victory. Another reason for the benevolence of Father Jap was perhaps the fact that the finish on the Alpe, one of the two highest on the Tour, is so close to Heaven, a factor that must benefit his parishioners as well as it seems to his compatriots from Holland. Perhaps this is also why the Alpe's priest overlooked any offence that he might have felt.

Offence, that is, that might have been felt because this was the first time that the Tour had broken with the old tradition of basing its organisation and the race media in the church of Notre-Dame-des-Neiges. After the church was judged too small and a bit too dark, the main body of the race was moved into the ski station's sports and cultural centre, a switch that was admirably carried out under the auspices of a former tennis player, Daniel Contet, the ideal person to oversee a switch of the Bastille Day ball. The July 14 party was held in the place where the Dutch had not only sent their champions, but also, it seemed, most of their population. The Alpe had the ambience of Munich on the evening of the European Nations Cup final, when Dutch football stars Ruud Gullit and Marco Van Basten had delivered a double of their own. Of course, we weren't in Bavaria, but the Dutch knocked the beer back as if we were and at such a speed that you'd be forgiven for believing that Amstel had laid a pipeline all the way here and was delivering the stuff at just the right pressure required to make it quaffable at an altitude of almost 2,000 metres.

Throughout the day, run from the green pastures of Chablais to the snowy summits of Oisans, there had been a long line of fans brandishing orange flags with a red, white and blue border and an ever-present shout as the race crossed through three valleys: "Hup! Hup! Hup! Holland!" These shouts of encouragement echoed back from the mountains like thunder, and the famous phrase uttered by the Viscount of Chateaubriand came to mind: "Raise yourselves from slumber, storms of desire." A theme that perhaps just might let itself to some sermonising by Father Jaap.

MICHEL CLARE
L'EQUIPE, JULY 15, 1988

14 JULY, 1981.
A 23-year-old new pro, Dutchman Peter Winnen, takes the stage having succeeded in dropping Bernard Hinault six kilometres from the summit. Winnen, who was 30 seconds clear with a kilometre remaining, managed to maintain eight seconds' advantage on Hinault and nine on Van Impe, and moved up to sixth place overall.

FOLLOW THE LEADER. In 1992, yellow jersey Miguel Indurain leads King of the Mountains Claudio Chiappucci on the Alpe, after Andy Hampsten has already gone clear to claim the first American success on the mountain.

Top left :
16 JULY, 1979. At the foot of Alpe d'Huez Joop Zoetemelk, after a viciously fast attack, has dropped Van Impe and Hinault. The yellow jersey, becoming an increasingly credible challenger, finishes 40 and 47 seconds respectively ahead of his rivals.

Middle left :
19 JULY, 1989. Theunisse flies towards victory towards the end of an extraordinary ride. At the same time Greg LeMond is hit by a sudden bout of weakness and Fignon regains the yellow jersey from him. The 'mano a mano' between the two champions continues.

Bottom left :
19 JULY, 1977. During a frightening confrontation with Bernard Thévenet, Hennie Kuiper throws all his efforts into going for victory and the yellow jersey. Although he obtains the first objective, he misses the second by eight seconds. But it was very close run thing for Thévenet.

Right :
14 JULY, 1988. Steven Rooks (left) produces a top drawer performance on the climb to Alpe d'Huez. He becomes the seventh Dutchman to win on the summit. As for Delgado (right), he must be content with third place after being beaten by Theunisse in the sprint. But he does take the yellow jersey.

Holland has found its mountain

On Alpe d'Huez, the Dutch are very much at home, thanks to a priest, a radio commentator and a line of great climbers.

ALPE D'HUEZ ISN'T A VOLCANO. It would be impossible to mimic the Neapolitans who turn Vesuvius into a huge censer by throwing smoke bombs the colour of Maradona's light sky blue Napoli shirt into its depths. When the Dutch came to this corner of the Alps they simply found a small village nestled beneath the peaks. They put up a cross and left a priest, Father Jaap Reuten, as if to claim ownership of the place. The Dutch used to prefer Bordeaux and slopes that would produce a decent wine rather than gradients that would strike fear into rouleurs and sprinters. But since the 1970s the Dutch have made the Alpe d'Huez stage their own. That was partly thanks to Theo Koomen, a commentator on the Dutch national radio channel, NOS, at the time. Harrie Janssen, his successor, confirms: "He romanticised the place. His broadcasts made the Dutch idolise this place. The ratings were incredible. And it wasn't just bike fans who were listening." So the Dutch, who have always appreciated the beauty of the Alps, looked at their road maps a little more closely and added a detour to this little corner of the Oisans region which has become a site of greatness.

STEFAN L'HERMITTE
L'EQUIPE, JULY 11, 1990

Left:
19 JULY, 1989. Gert-Jan Theunisse wants to assure himself of the King of the Mountains jersey. He attacks on the Croix-de-Fer and, to his great surprise, no one joins him. At the finish he explains why he was so determined to defend his advantage: "Alpe d'Huez is a bit like Holland in France, isn't it?"

Right:
20 JULY, 1982. More than a minute and a half behind the Swiss Breu (winner), Alban (second), Fernandez (third) and Martin (fourth), the big guns arrive: Hinault is flanked by the orange guard of Zoetemelk (left) and Winnen (right). But at Alpe d'Huez Hinault confirms his yellow jersey.

1986: HINAULT AND LEMOND CREATE HISTORY

It's the end of a fabulous stage, and Bernard Hinault and Greg LeMond have put their differences aside. It has been made-for-television stuff. The two La Vie Claire team-mates have relegated their main rival, Urs Zimmermann, to third place in the overall classification, nearly eight minutes down. But the Tour still isn't over!

"At the start of this race, I had said that as it's a Tour made for climbers we were really going to see them show themselves," Hinault says. He seems pretty pleased with himself, but he's got the right to be. After dealing with the world's media he's taken shelter in a Coca-Cola publicity van, where the French minister for sport, M. Bergelin, is waiting for him. With him are Greg LeMond, Jean-François Bernard, Michel Hidalgo and Bernard Tapie.

This morning, like every morning, the La Vie Claire team had plotted how they would dominate the stage. And today it was all about how to bring down Zimmermann. But by the end of the day it was Hinault taking the stage win, the combativity prize, the prize of number one team member and the best rouleur trophy. Yesterday he was suffering with his knee, but today he's taken Zimm apart. "Yesterday evening, after the stage, I underwent meso-therapy," a process by which a needle is used to make lots of little holes to let the medicine filter directly through into the injured area, explains Hinault. "I was a bit worried about my knee at the foot of the Croix-de-Fer," he says. "I was wondering just how hard I could push it, but it held out all right. And as for Zimmermann, well..." To make life as hard as possible for those climbers, Hinault had to be right up at the front of the race.

"They're thin – they've got no reserves," he explains. "And so you have to attack them until there's nothing more they can do, until they're not able to recover sufficiently. It's easy to do." It certainly sounds simple enough. Barring accidents, it would seem that for Zimmermann this Tour has been lost even before starting the terrible climb to the top of Alpe d'Huez. Its slopes are packed with people waiting. It's an enthusiastic, but rebellious and hostile crowd: they're not willing to accept that Hinault's chances in this race are being sacrificed for Greg LeMond. "That was not acceptable for them to be that way, because at one point Greg told me that he was scared," Hinault says. The American agrees, and seems disappointed in the public for having acted in such a manner.

As the two riders approach the summit, they're hand in hand. Bernard doesn't forget, though, even in such an emotional moment, to push just that little bit harder on the pedals - enough to give him the stage victory. "I told Greg that I wanted to win the stage." And the American didn't argue. "I'm proud of what we've done together," continues Hinault, "but again, the Tour isn't over yet. Who's the stronger out of the two of us in the mountains? You'll have to ask Greg! I haven't gifted him this Tour de France. This Tour is a gift for the team. By finishing here hand in hand, I think we've given everyone a fantastic image of the sport."

Once again Hinault has shown us what he can do. He's taken Fignon, Herrera, Millar and Zimmermann out of the equation. All of his rivals except for his team-mate. What will Hinault do tomorrow? The situation reminds me of the film Vera Cruz, an old Gary Cooper and Burt Lancaster western. The two heroes out to find the treasure, but who, together, must first beat the bad guys. Then the day comes when the two of them stand face to face over the treasure. And then it's all about whoever can draw first.

Vera Cruz and Alpe d'Huez are almost the same thing. But Greg LeMond, in the lead, wearer of the yellow jersey, wants peace. And Hinault? "Now that it's just the two of us, perhaps we can fight it out between us," he says with a devilish smile. Certainly he is not going to let LeMond take the Golden Fleece without a fight. But today the race belonged to La Vie Claire. Tomorrow is another day.

ERIC LAHMY

L'EQUIPE, JULY 22, 1986

JULY 21, 1986.
The image of the 1986 Tour de France: LeMond and Hinault cross the finish line hand in hand. There was no sprint between the two team-mates. Instead LeMond eases off but keeps the yellow jersey.

Hunter turned gamekeeper

Writer, singer, and journalist for L'Equipe during the Tour de France, Jean Amadou has been 'fooled' by the spectacle.

LIKE TRAGEDY OR COMEDY, the epic has its own strict rules, with its own particular characters and set of circumstances. In the one written yesterday on the slopes of the Oisans region, the performance of the Breton, Hinault, and the American, LeMond, will stay in the memory and appear in the books just like all the Tour legends before them. Everyone's talking about it - and even those who are normally difficult to impress have been moved by the riders' exploits.

I am a man who appreciates such a spectacle. I love it when someone can pull it off, no matter what field it's in. And Bernard Hinault has understood for a long time that in cycling there is a need for such panache to stir and excite the public. He won't have forgotten that the best welcome a rider arriving in Paris has ever received was that which greeted Poulidor in a Tour which he had lost, but where he had supported, protected and advised Pingeon, who was barely able to hold onto the yellow jersey in the high mountains.

At Alpe d'Huez, Hinault jumped even further up the popularity scale as the hunter turned gamekeeper. By acting as the American's mentor, Hinault underlined his perfect understanding of what it takes to trigger the crowd's enthusiasm. And whatever happens, he's won in the public's eyes: if he wins the Tour, he's a hero; if he loses, he's an idol.

My natural scepticism means that I should be suspicious of top riders' hugging and kissing of each other, just when the cameras are pointing in their direction. I suspect a touch of affectation. Yet when Hinault and LeMond fell into each other's arms on the podium, it seemed to me that the gesture was spontaneous. Despite everything that I've seen before and the cynicism that's built up in me, the Tour has restored a feeling of naivety that had long since been dulled.

JEAN AMADOU
L'EQUIPE, JULY 21, 1986

Above left:
ON THE COL DE LA CROIX-DE-FER, Hinault and LeMond ride away from Ruiz-Cabestany...

Above right:
...AND ARE LEFT ALONE IN THE LEAD, nearly three minutes ahead of the Zimmermann group...

...ON THE DESCENT OF THE COL DE LA CROIX-DE-FER, the two riders increase the gap back to Zimmermann. By the finish at Alpe d'Huez they are more than five minutes ahead of the Swiss.

YVON MADIOT (left), Criquiélion (with bottle) and Ruttiman (right) battle it out further down the road behind Hinault and LeMond.

FRENCH CHAMPION Yvon Madiot, riding well from the beginning of the stage to the end, finishes fifth on the day.

THE SWISS, Urs Zimmermann is the big loser of the day.

ON THE APPROACH TO THE FINISH, in front of a huge crowd, Greg LeMond and Bernard Hinault make it look easy. Their epic performance is coming to its end.

L'EQUIPE, July 22, 1986.

IT'S A SYMBOLIC IMAGE: as
the two team-mates arrive
together at the finish, it's just
Bernard Hinault you can see... and
the shadow of LeMond behind him.

GRANDS CHAMPIONS AND GREAT DUELS

From Coppi and Robic in 1952 to Armstrong and Ullrich in 2001 via Hinault and Fignon in 1984, Thévenet and Kuiper in 1977 and LeMond and Fignon in 1989, Alpe d'Huez has always been the stage for epic duels between supreme champions who have enriched the history of the Tour de France. However, after 22 visits to the ski station only twice has the winner here gone on to win the Tour: Fausto Coppi in 1952 and Lance Armstrong in 2001.

The legend of Alpe d'Huez began with the exploits of two great riders. It was 1952 and the first time the mountain featured in the Tour, and the people's champion of post-war France, Jean 'Biquet' Robic, attacked just after Bourg d'Oisans, daring to defy the great Fausto Coppi. But the 'Campionissimo' couldn't be beaten as easily as that, and took his time to reel in the insolent Breton before blowing him away.

Since then, some of the biggest duels of the Tour have been played out over the 21 hairpin bends on the Alpe's slopes. In 1984, as the Colombian Luis Herrera led up the mountain, sending Bogota hysterical with joy, what was going through Bernard Hinault's head as he was dropped by the 24-year-old Laurent Fignon? The Breton had given his attack in the valley everything, only for the Parisian to later say that the attack had "made me laugh." And as Fignon rode away from him, perhaps some of Hinault's youth went away with him too.

But 'the Badger' was not finished with the Alpe. Who could forget 1986 when, in an emotional end to the stage, Hinault crossed the finish line hand in hand with his young American team-mate at Bernard Tapie's La Vie Claire team, Greg LeMond? Yes, LeMond went on to win the Tour that year, but Hinault - declared winner of the stage - couldn't have wished for a better farewell to the sport.

Then in that crazy Tour of 1989 it was again LeMond in yellow. The Alpe d'Huez stage that year was especially memorable for its atmosphere. The crowds were so big that they left just a narrow corridor for the riders, and the yellow jersey was swallowed up in a sea of people. But somehow Fignon's directeur sportif, Cyrille Guimard, suddenly decided that LeMond was in trouble. "Come on!" Guimard barked at Fignon. In response Fignon could only pull a face. "Come on, he's finished..." He knew Greg

LeMond by heart because he had been the American rider's manager for a number of years. And for the third time, the yellow jersey was waiting at the top of the Alpe for Fignon to make it his. "Whoever has the yellow jersey at the summit of Alpe d'Huez," they'd said, "will have won the Tour..." That was certainly the case for Fignon in both 1983 and 1984, but not this time. Or rather it was. Fignon took the jersey and wore it all the way to Paris, only to lose it on the Champs Elysées by those famous eight seconds.

In 1976 Alpe d'Huez was the setting for the shoulder-to-shoulder battle between Van Impe and Zoetemelk. The Dutchman, Zoetemelk, took the stage, while the Belgian, Van Impe, took the Tour. The same Van Impe, in 1977, attacked, then cracked, then fell, knocked over by a following car, while Bernard Thévenet rode himself to his absolute limits in containing the spirited riding of Hennie Kuiper. And then it was Zoetemelk, again, in 1979 putting up a great fight against Bernard Hinault - the year when the riders had to climb Alpe d'Huez two days in a row.

For Miguel Indurain, defending his first yellow jersey in 1991, it was the ultimate test. Gianni Bugno, in winning the stage for the second year in a row, had left all of his rivals standing. All except one. Miguel Indurain hadn't wavered, and was beaten by just one second on the line. What a match again in 1995: Indurain, 1.88 metres tall and 79 kilos, against Marco Pantani, 1.72 metres and 56 kilos. And of course, the big Spaniard, in spite of his great presence, is again just too polite to assert himself. Alpe d'Huez will always remain a climber's paradise.

PHILIPPE BOUVET

JULY 16, 1984
and Laurent Fignon rides away from Bernard Hinault after a memorable battle. Fignon is still about 50 seconds behind the Colombian 'Lucho' Herrera, who gives his country their first success in the Tour de France.

JULY 19, 1977.
An extremely
aggravated Bernard
Thévenet 'tows' the
Dutchmen Zoetemelk
and Kuiper (left), who
will go on to win the
stage.

JULY 4, 1976. Lucien
Van Impe (left) yields
at the summit to Joop
Zoetemelk (right), but
still takes the yellow
jersey.

16 JULY, 1979. The dazzling Zoetemelk attempts and carries off a real coup de grace. At the summit of the Alpe he finishes ahead of Van Impe (left) and Hinault.

1979: Zoetemelk revolts

Joop Zoetemelk challenged the superiority of Bernard Hinault with panache.

TO NOT KNOW WHEN TO GIVE IN, EVEN when everything seems lost and to provoke an adversary who is clearly superior without taking into account the risks run by doing so are both essential qualities of a champion and characteristics that Joop Zoetemelk can pride himself on. Long ago, the Baron de Coubertin stressed the need for athletes to push themselves as far as they can, this being the only that they can avoid self-recrimination in the face of failure, and the only honourable way of ensuring they receive the respect of others.

It's not known whether Zoetemelk, a man committed to his profession, had the time to read the works of the baron, but we like to imagine him being there in amongst the enormous crowd on the Alpe tipping his hat in respect as the man in the green jersey passes by, and perhaps offering him a friendly wave with his cane. It wouldn't have escaped the eye of the man who founded the Olympic Games that under the skin of this man hardened by his experience in all of the world's great cycling events beats the heart of one of de Coubertin's much-prized amateurs. The baron would have appreciated the extraordinary effort made by Bernard Hinault's last rival, an effort that was both an act of revolt and a cry of liberation at the same time.

In the end it might have been pointless from the racing perspective, but Joop Zoetemelt certainly picked up the gauntlet thrown down at him, not by the man in the yellow jersey, but by a critical public who have accused him of being economical with his effort, of being too prudent, of being unable to put together a winning hand. However, Zoetemelk staked everything on one single hand by taking the initiative at the foot of Alpe d'Huez, even though he must surely have thought that his rival was totally without lacking in weaknesses. He must have known, professional that he is, that the least error in his strategy, the least slip in the face of unforeseen events, would lead to another failure, which would only have added to his rival's prestige. Having been around a bit, he would also have known that another defeat would have given rise to sarcastic comments such as: "Poor old Joop, he's a good sort, but he hasn't really got the right stuff." All that he could have hoped for in engaging in a battle like this where he could not foresee the result would be an enthusiastic welcome on the Champs Elysées, no matter what the colour of his jersey.

PIERRE CHANY
L'EQUIPE, JULY 17, 1979

1984: Sublime and cruel

Herrera is victorious, Fignon is superb, Hinault comes unstuck and LeMond recovers. What a stage!

ON THE INTERMINABLE CLIMB UP ALPE D'HUEZ, to which hordes of people cling bearing the colours of every country under the sun, the Tour de France offered both sublime entertainment and extreme cruelty. The sublime came in both the frail and dark shape of Luis Herrera, the conqueror of Colombian summits who replied with brio to the demands of his distant compatriots, and of Laurent Fignon, the French champion, whose horizons expand every day as he imposes his iron rule on the international challengers for his title.

The former regained for the climbers, the legendary heroes of the Tour, their rightful glory as he finished 49 seconds ahead of the man who would take over the yellow jersey where he had received it the previous year. The cruelty was reserved for Bernard Hinault, a real scrapper, a proud rider and a man always looking for a challenge, who offered himself up with admirable generosity. In an attempt to blow the stage apart and test Laurent Fignon's limits, Hinault ended up enduring absolute agony during the last hour of the stage. During a champion's career, the cruellest moment comes when they realise the extent of their weakness in the face of the attacks of insolent youth, and it would seem that the former world champion arrived at that moment today. He will always have a place in this great event, but today he lost almost three minutes to Fignon - 2-55 to be exact.

It seems that he will now have to hand over his powers of leadership to the man who has clearly shown himself a worthy successor as unquestioned king of the road. What was an intense day of racing from every aspect loudly confirmed the spectacular rise of the French champion, who has shown his domination four times since the start of the race, and has also confirmed the limits of the Breton. He's not without speed on the climbs, but that speed isn't now enough to allow him to stay with the best, and neither does it allow him to carry out his ambitious strategies.

On this mountain battered by the wind, where the crowd allows the riders just the narrowest of passages, Hinault finished a sad day in a state close to distress, but he never gives up the fight and already has plans for revenge for today, tomorrow and the days after: "Today I've been thrashed. But I won't stop attacking before Paris!" he vowed 10 minutes after the finish.

PIERRE CHANY
L'EQUIPE, JULY 17, 1984

L'ÉQUIPE, July 17, 1984.

JULY 16, 1984.
The Tour tips in one rider's favour: Bernard Hinault has put up a brave fight but he can't stay with the superb Laurent Fignon, who goes ahead to claim the yellow jersey. The distant Herrera takes a historic victory for Colombia.

1989: Chin up, LeMond

Four kilometres from the summit, LeMond was still in the company of Fignon and Delgado. But then, without warning, he blew up and was dropped, and his two rivals were not going to hang around and wait for him.

THEUNISSE HAD BLOWN AWAY ALL OF THOSE who had tried to stay with him, then held off everybody as he flew through the valley, his long hair flapping in the wind, and prevented Millar, Bugno, Cornillet and Pino of having any hope of getting back up to him on the slopes of the Alpe. He had been relentless in his riding all day, although his lead had never got up to much more than four minutes. Not enough to shake up the Tour, but more than enough to win the most prestigious stage of the race.

On the road behind him, everything was set for a grand finale to this Tour. "Whoever has the yellow jersey at the summit of Alpe d'Huez," they'd said that morning, "will have won the Tour." In another Tour maybe, but not in this one. The jersey, at the start of the climb - 21 hairpin bends from the top - is safely on the wide shoulders of Greg LeMond. And looking at LeMond's legs and his breathing, he doesn't appear to be suffering. It was him who responded immediately when Fignon accelerated at hairpin number 20, with Delgado a little slower to react. But now it's time for Abelardo Rondon - one of the principal players of this Tour - to buckle down and start helping his Reynolds leader, Delgado, his legs turning a hellish cadence for the best part of eight kilometres. Soon the group has been whittled down to just five riders: Rondon, Delgado, LeMond, Fignon, Lejarreta. And then Lejarreta cracks: they're down to four.

On one of the bends, an outstretched hand offers up a bottle of water. In this heat on Alpe d'Huez, where everything burns - your skin as much as your lungs - a bottle of water is simply irresistible. Rondon sprays the water on himself and passes the bottle to 'Perico' Delgado, who turns and offers the bottle to LeMond, who passes it on to Fignon.

The road seems to have disappeared - a sea of people now covers it. Still it's Rondon on the front, setting such a pace that Delgado doesn't even have time to think about an attack. With just five kilometres to go, the Tour is surely finished - LeMond is still there. What can Guimard possibly do, from the third car in the line, to make sure that it isn't so? Somehow managing to part the crowds, the Super U directeur sportif is suddenly alongside Fignon: "Come on!" In response Fignon can only pull a face.

"Come on, he's finished."

LeMond is finished. And only Guimard has seen it. He knows, having been the American rider's manager for many years, the signs to look for: that when LeMond loses his rhythm, that's it. "When he sits down, stands up, sits down again, it's because he's cracked. And when Greg cracks, he really cracks." That, Guimard knows by heart. Fignon listens to his directeur's words, and they make him believe that suddenly anything is possible. It would be really terrible if Fignon had to let this opportunity pass. And if it's Guimard who's telling him it's time, then Fignon knows that he must go for it.

And he does, at four kilometres exactly from the summit. Delgado's with him immediately. LeMond sits down again, desperately trying to rediscover his rhythm, rolling his shoulders. The crowds close in around him. LeMond can't react. For five hundred metres, it's awful. The yellow jersey is drowning in amongst the hordes of people, and none of the cars and none of

JULY 19, 1989. Theunisse has already flown, and Delgado, Alcala, Bugno, LeMond, Fignon and Rondon are in pursuit.

the motorbikes can get close enough to him to open up the crowds. Now it is courage that is driving this Tour. "You know, Laurent hasn't been great in this Tour," Guimard says later. "I saw that he was great in the Giro, but here it's been more about having the guts to really ride."

But LeMond has guts, too: he's recovered and is riding better again. He has the yellow jersey by 53 seconds and he has to defend it. With two kilometres to go, Fignon and Delgado have taken 52 of them exactly. At this point of the climb of Alpe d'Huez there is a bit of a false flat - perhaps a last chance for LeMond, who can now shift up a gear or two.

But as he crosses the line, the gap is one minute and nine seconds. Just like the other day at Superbagnères, he's lost the yellow jersey - this time by 26 seconds. And 26 seconds will be virtually impossible to get back in Sunday's 24.5-kilometre time trial from Versailles to Paris - around a second a kilometre. But even before he's got his breath back, LeMond is already talking about making up lost time at Villard-de-Lans, or tomorrow at Aix-les-Bains. And who would dare to say that Delgado is out of this Tour yet either?

PHILIPPE BOUVET
L'EQUIPE, JULY 20, 1989

GERT-JAN THEUNISSE crossed the line a minute and nine seconds before Pedro Delgado beats Laurent Fignon for second. With a lead of 26 seconds, Fignon is the new race leader. "Who will win the Tour?" is the headline in L'Equipe on July 20. No one knows yet.

23 JULY, 1991. Gianni Bugno follows Miguel Indurain, who's been very impressive on the climb...

...THE ITALIAN TRIES TO ATTACK to shake off the Spanish champion, who responds...

LUC LEBLANC, who's been held up after a collision with a spectator, gets back up to the lead group...

...A HUGE CROWD URGES on the three leaders just short of the finish line where Bugno will repeat his success of the previous year by coming in ahead of Indurain and Leblanc.

THE GIANTS OF THE ROAD GET CARRIED ALONG BY THE CROWD

Come the Tour, it's always the same on Alpe d'Huez. Exactly how many people are there in the great 14km long tide that engulfs the climb? Maybe 100,000, maybe more. It's free entry for all and no one is keeping count. One stat you can work out though is that if you leave the mountain at 11 in the evening, when all the day's festivities have finally wound down, it's likely to take you until four the next morning to make it to Grenoble, less than 80km away.

All the way up the road, there's a mad mix of painted letters, new words painted over old, like a crazed crossword. You can make out some of it, slogans devoted to the Canadian Steve Bauer, France's Thierry Claveyrolat or Italy's Gianni Bugno. But the champion graffiti-writers on the mountain are, for some reason, the ones writing in Dutch. The names of Rooks, Winnen and even Theunisse, the great lost hope, are still cherished by the faithful and are scattered all over the roads. And there's one more name scrawled all the way from the bottom of the mountain right up to the final bend: Febo. Febo? Not the nickname of some up-and-coming cycling hero, but the name of a hamburger stall owned by a man called Rob. "I had a lot of help doing all that," he laughs, reflecting on the string of namechecks all the way up the mountain. "There's nothing like free publicity…"

A cart with a chocolate nun on top stops five yards in front of him. The caravane publicitaire passes. Two friends have perched their chairs on the roof of their caravan. "People don't come just for the bikes," says Rob. "You come here for a holiday. No women, no children, no phones. For a week, you can become a child again…"

The crowds have been building up since Sunday: men, generally, telling each other that life without the family, at least for a few days, is really rather good. Between their two vans, Rob and Ron have a table full of food. Rob is stuffing his face. Ron, a grey-haired man, is in the van getting some more rolls. Meanwhile, the Witschge family – a father and his two sons – are talking about football, and Ajax in particular. "We invite everyone when we come here," he says. "Some years, there's about 30 of us."

For 10 years now, this little corner of Oisans has been the heart of their kingdom. This year, the Dutch flag is not flying quite so high on Alpe d'Huez. Theunisse isn't riding this year; some fans have chosen the world championships for their annual jaunt this time round, rather than come to the Tour; for others, it's even a little early in the year. But the Witschges have a lifetime season-ticket to the Alpe. And although the climb's most exciting turns have been cleared and the fans forced to vent their passion in a car park, well, it'd take more than that to dampen their fervour. The voices are rising now. The riders are here: LeMond in the rainbow jersey, Bugno in red and black; then, behind, Breukink – their man Breukink. Tonight, there'll be a new name on their roll call of champions, a new name to rank alongside the Kuipers and Zoetemelks and Rooks and Theunisses. The fans have been willing this kind of ending for days. Rob raises his hat and gives out a huge cheer. He knows that he's a winner whatever happens to their man further up the mountain: "Win or lose, it's all the same to us," says the hot-dog seller. "People always need to eat…"

STEFAN L'HERMITTE
L'EQUIPE, JULY 12, 1990

AT THE STEEPEST POINT OF THE CLIMB, the never-ending wait in the summer sun is over as the peloton's advance party finally comes into view. With the roar of the crowd and the din of the motorbikes and support cars, the mountain seems in the grip of mania. In such a cauldron, the (holy) water comes like a blessed relief for Marco Pantani.

Right:
SOMETIMES IT CAN BE AGGRESSIVE, but the crowd can also be charming – as Stéphane Heulot discovers.

Far right:
NO OTHER SPORT takes its champion so close to his public. Four kilometres from home, the fervour of the crowd is ringing in Marco Pantani's ears as he pushes for home.

LED BY THE KING, Miguel Indurain, the lead group surge up through the baying throng. On this road anyone can release their emotions in any way they want.

MARCO PANTANI FIGHTS HIS WAY THROUGH THE FOUR-DEEP spectators on Alpe d'Huez – riders don't see daylight until the crowds part at the last possible moment.

FROM LAURENT FIGNON to Greg LeMond in the yellow jersey to all the other water-carriers, the riders head for the summit through the fans' guard of honour.

ALL THE WAY UP THE ROAD people from all over Europe are eating and sleeping and living and waiting, waiting for what seems like forever for their heroes. The publicity caravan is a big part of a spectacle that lasts both a matter of moments and a whole day.

The untimely postman

Novelist – and L'Equipe special correspondent – Jacques Perret declared himself a particular fan of one cyclist at Alpe d'Huez...

THE SUN WAS SHINING ON the valley. Down there, the riders were going along in sensible groups, keeping their powder dry for Alpe d'Huez later in the day. The Midi sun was bubbling the tar on the roads and the peloton was whirring along, with team-mates elbow to elbow, having the odd word with each other about the weather or the odd bit of gossip. The motorbike riders, already covered in dust, were standing up on their bikes and peering towards the horizon. It was midday, and everything was peaceful.

Peaceful that is apart from a village postman heading slowly towards the peloton from the opposite direction, pedalling with the calm assurance of a man who makes this journey every single day. The road was cleared hours ago, cleared for the icons of the sport, but the postman doesn't care about all that: he carries on regardless riding towards the peloton as the roadside gendarmes whistle in vain to stop him. He was just going about his business, hat on the side of his head, with his regulation satchel, on his standard-issue bike. Nothing was going to stop him.

When he spots the peloton rearing up towards him out of nowhere, he seems to hesitate and weigh up the strange and unusual sight before him. As abuse and advice rains in from all sides in every language imaginable, he just carries on his heroic way, blowing kisses here and there, zig-zagging and riding against the flow, pushing his old bike ever onwards for the glory of the postal service.

I wouldn't want to take anything away from the official race standings and especially not from everything that Fausto Coppi did here – but I'd just like to award my own personal palmarès to my postman, to fete him like some kind of champion. For me, for a moment, he surpassed anything the peloton could do.

He gave a bravura display of individualism. He took up the gauntlet on an old bike with one gear, supported by neither team nor publicity agents nor roadside crowds or any of the technical advances of the last 50 years.

OK, so the man was in the wrong. But if ever anyone deserved the 'most combative rider' award, it was the cheeky postman.

JACQUES PERRET
L'EQUIPE, JULY 4, 1952.

Above from left to right:
THE END OF A DAY'S SUFFERING in sight for Fignon and Delgado, 1989.

MIGUEL INDURAIN and Alex Zülle on the Alpe. A charming route but full of danger...

AS THE RIDERS BATTLE UPWARDS, the spectators select the route for them, forcing them from one side of the road to the other and back again.

IN ONES AND TWOS, in groups big and small, the Tour riders get the same fantastic reception. The crowds make no distinction between the peloton's patron and the also-rans, between their own favourites and the others. Here, Germany's Jan Ullrich is roared on by Dutch fans.

MIGUEL INDURAIN IS THE CHAMPION IN YELLOW, Gianni Bugno the challenger, and there's Joe Public at the side of the road: everyone becomes a bit player next to the star of the show, the Alpe itself.

A PUNISHING INCLINE, SUFFERING ON THE ALPE

The evening after Luis Herrera of Colombia's historic win in 1984, Jean Amadou looked back over how one of the peloton's more lowly footsoldiers had spent the day. A day of graft in the face of general indifference. A day spent a long long way behind the peloton's champions, in the shadow of exhaustion. A day when the roars of the crowd sound like an act of sympathy. A day when you have to dig deep to find the strength to dream of a brighter future.

Under the unforgiving sun, he climbed. Climbed 13 kilometres and 21 corners of loose stones. He didn't see the crowds at all as waves of sound crashed around his ears. Tall and gangling, his face long with prominent cheekbones, he had come up the col du Coq as part of a single file procession, his eyes fixed to the back wheel of the rider in front, ears deaf to all but the hypnotic crunch of tyres on the asphalt. No words are spoken. The directeur sportif had talked to him about the route beforehand, told him the plan. He respects the directeur: the directeur gives the orders, and talks about things the rider isn't even aware of. He's done his bit today, always looking to get in any breaks, fetching and carrying the bidons for the star riders, helping bring the stragglers back to the bunch. But now he is all alone, his arms at full stretch on his handlebars, struggling for air despite the pure mountain air. He can feel his own warm breath on his face. He feels his lungs shrinking, like a giant has taken them into one enormous fist and crushed them.

"What a job," he mutters to himself. He climbs. He gets angry with himself for his choice of employment. He climbs some more. The others, the stars, may already be on the podium at the top. They've had a good day. The French Revolution hasn't done anything for me, he thinks, still a slave to a master. Why shouldn't he be the one at the front? He could be in yellow, he could be a star, he could be on the podium, being interviewed and being given flowers and getting kissed by fresh-faced young girls. Why not? It's all running round his head feverishly as the road gets steeper and steeper. The fans - idiots, all idiots - cry out "Come on" like words could make his job any easier. He wants to tell them to push him instead of cheering him - but he doesn't dare. The suggestion dies in his throat, strangled by a humbleness that dates right back to childhood, a reticence that overcomes him whenever it comes to asking for something he really wants. The incline gets even steeper. This is all he needs. Now, he'd like to stop. To get off and finish on foot, ignoring all the jeering and laughing of the crowd. He rages at the race directors who chose the stage route, propped up in their seats at the summit, without any consideration for his suffering. It's always the same - the strong asserting themselves over the weak without a second thought.

If he was well paid for this drudgery then it might all be worth it. Worth putting in the hours in return for a few pence thrown from the sides like he was some kind of beggar. He carries on climbing the crumbling road to the accompaniment of his ragged breathing. The July sun roasts the road. His suffering and misery is bigger than the mountain is tall. One day, he will have his moment. He'll be up there on the podium, the weak will overcome the strong. The Fignons and Hinaults will be slogging their guts out at the back. And he'll take the yellow jersey, overflowing with joy at the end of a dream day, as the sun sets perfectly in the mountain sky.

JEAN AMADOU
L'EQUIPE, JULY 17, 1984

THE FINISH LINE CHANGES EVERYTHING. The champion is assaulted by fatigue. Exhausted, his breathing gets quicker, his muscles harden even before they get some much-needed attention. In 1976, at the end of the first climb of the Alpe in the modern era, Raymond Poulidor is among the first of the exhausted to the summit.

The incredible becomes commonplace

The Tour de France, and especially Alpe d'Huez, are inextricably linked with superhuman achievement. Mundanity is simply out of the question.

THE TOUR DE FRANCE has become a phenomenon that thrives on exaggerated feats of heroism. It leaves an indelible impression. The riders fly by as if on motor-bikes in an awe-inspiring cavalcade, dazzling the public, who are temporarily removed from the mundanity of everyday existence.

The Tour's ability to remove any care in the world is why even the most po-faced of visitors can be swept back to a state of child-like wonder when following the race in a car. A feeling of excess, a lack of control even, takes over as the madness of the event and the crazed commentary on the radios remove all sense of reality and reduce the whole event to a phrase most often associated with kids: "It's brilliant."

Bizarrely, sometimes cycling and its champions lose centre stage to the technicians whose efforts on the ground and in the air bring the whole event to us, and who the commentators almost go as far as comparing to Indurain. There's a symbiotic relationship here between the Tour and television, the former allowing the latter to promote and package the whole mad affair, while the media eulogise the superhuman achievements on display with the aim of boosting their spellbound audience.

If anyone were to dare to admit that cycling isn't the toughest sport in the world it would be no surprise to see the men with the white coats appear and take them away to be quarantined and treated for their clear delusion. And this despite the fact that we get so carried away that some commentators might even say that the helicopters hovering over Alpe d'Huez are more exposed to danger than those that flitted over the highlands around Sarajevo in the midst of that region's conflict.

The desire to over-dramatise can affect anyone travelling with the race and effectively not living in the real world. Imaginations run riot and everyone is driven to embellish every little incident they see. Consequently, the Tour encourages a bizarre relationship between the public on one side who never cease with their shouts of encouragement, while on the other side the race's camp-followers feel that they have to divorce themselves from all thoughts of reality.

Anything that is run of the mill is overlooked as those in the race caravan become intoxicated with repeating over and over: "It really is incredible." This tendency to over-exaggerate enables the public to grasp the extent of the huge suffering being endured by the giants of the road, suffering that becomes greater than ever on the slopes of Alpe d'Huez. It makes the riders a race apart, raised to a higher level by those who shout for them from the side of the road or sing their praises on the TV, radio and in the papers.

CHRISTIAN MONTAIGNAC
L'EQUIPE, JULY 13, 1995

Left :
IN 1979, watched by TV commentator Robert Chapatte, Bernard Hinault finds out that you need to give your all to conquer Alpe d'Huez.

Far Right :
ROBERT ALBAN suffers on the unforgiving ascent in 1982. The effort required is intense and absolute. Alpe d'Huez takes from everyone - and gives back to a select few.

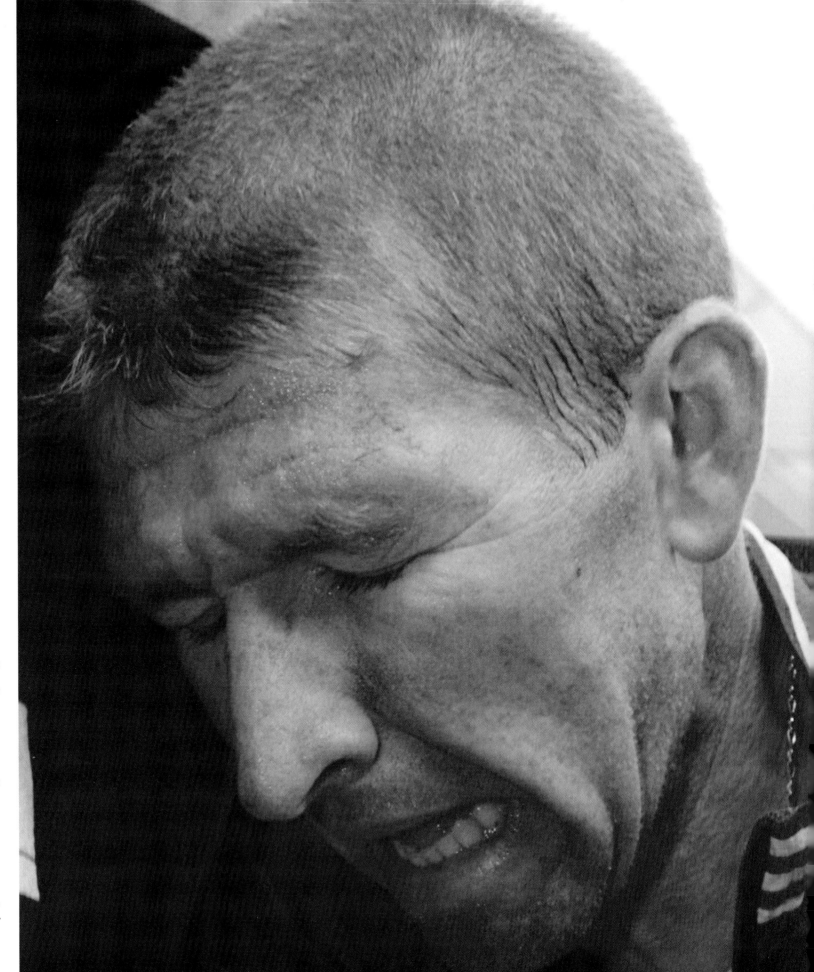

Right :
IN 2001, Francois Simon is on the verge of passing out as he crosses the line. Winning the yellow jersey is some compensation for his efforts, though...

Far Right :
AN EXHAUSTED Michel Pollentier crosses the line first in 1978 - but the happiest day of his career would soon turn very sour, as he was caught trying to cheat a dope test with a bizarre contraption strapped to his body and designed to deceive the dope control.

Don't forget the 'gruppetto'

On every mountain stage, the non-climbers get together to make up the 'gruppetto' and help each other round. One of their number, Jacky Durand, explains.

"WHY NOT GO FOR HOME FROM A LONG WAY OUT and try to win the Bastille Day stage at the summit of Alpe d'Huez?" The idea came to Jacky Durand last winter during a training camp in the mountains with his Lotto team. No French rider can ignore the special feelings of the French national day, especially not a two-time French champion. Even riding for the Belgian team Lotto, Durand's patriotism burns. But there's a big divide between what seems like a good idea in the middle of winter and the truth of the situation seven months later. Durand found out exactly how big that gulf was as soon as the Tour hit the first hairpin in the mountains. Durand suffered a blow to his pride early on the stage to Sestrières. We were right at the start of a long stage that would see the most extreme weather conditions. There was still the Galibier to come and then the long climb to Sestrières itself. Dropped already and with over 100 kilometres to go, Durand didn't hesitate: he set about rounding up some likely candidates for the day's 'gruppetto'.

The day before yesterday Durand was turning his head a lot, looking behind him at the looming broom wagon. But he managed to save himself from being swept up by getting inside the time limit by eight minutes. Yesterday, the realisation that the profile of the stage to Alpe d'Huez bore no relation at all to his winter daydream hit Durand hard. The climb of Mont Cenis was enough to put his notions of Bastille Day glory on the back-burner. When his companion, the courageous Raivis Belohvosckis, the lanterne rouge at the start of the day, decided to climb off after 55km, Durand promptly opted for the safety net he had found refuge in the previous day. The 'gruppetto' had gone off without him on the toughest part of the climb just as the Lotto team was in the middle of a great drama. Jos Braeckevelt, team manager Jean-Luc Vandenbroucke's assistant, had just smoked his last cigar. It was going to be a long day for Lotto.

But Durand has plenty of guts. Fighting back, he came up to Axel Merckx first, whose father Eddy had perhaps not chosen the best day to be watching his son. After 71km, the Mapei rider got off. "I'm spent," he said as he got into the directeur sportif's car. "It's impossible to carry on like this. If I'd known before how my form would be I wouldn't feel so bad."

The Tour doctor diagnosed Merckx with a stomach complaint. Meanwhile, Durand was soldiering on, taking on the terrible Croix-de-Fer climb. The former French champion's eyes were always fixed on the hairpin above, on his colleagues in the gruppetto. A number of them, Svorada, Van Bon, Padrnos and Savoldelli decided to follow the fireworks on the Alpe in civilian rather than cycling kit. Dekker then came up to Durand like a rocket thanks to a firm handsling from his directeur sportif, and Durand managed to get back up to the group with him as they crossed the Oisans valley before tackling the last torturous incline of the day. By the foot of the climb the directeurs sportifs had consulted and decided it was better for one gruppetto to start up the Alpe than two smaller pelotons.

At the first of the 21 turns on the climb, there were 87 brave souls hanging in together just wanting to get home within the time limit. Jacky Durand was one of them. His yo-yo drama was not over, though. He cracked again just before the 10km to go banner, just as Giuseppe Guerini crossed the finishing line all the way up the mountain. But what's 10 kilometres climbing for Jacky Durand, especially on Bastille Day when you've already got 200 kilometres of torture behind you? Yesterday, he made it a point of honour to finish somehow, holding onto the coat-tails of the gruppetto and came home second to last. You don't get rid of Jacky Durand that easily.

MANUEL MARTINEZ
L'EQUIPE, JULY 15, 1999

Above, left to right :
ON THIS JULY DAY IN 1989 Laurent Fignon goes right to the limit in the effort to distance his great rival, Greg LeMond.

2001: Jan Ullrich seems to have aged almost visibly as he completes the exhausting stage to the summit.

JOSEBA BELOKI, apparently welded to his saddle after the epic ascent in the searing sun, also in 2001.

EVEN YELLOW JERSEYS don't escape the wrath of Alpe d'Huez. Ronan Pensec, ready to drop as he faces the press in 1990.

GREEN JERSEY Laurent Jalabert still in recovery some minutes after finishing in 1995.

2001: LANCE ARMSTRONG ACHIEVES HIS DREAM

Setting off on his own at the foot of Alpe d'Huez, Lance Armstrong distanced himself from all of his main rivals, leaving the most dangerous of them, Jan Ullrich, more than two minutes behind. Strangely subdued during the day's first two climbs, it seems he was playing a remarkable game of deception with the active complicity of his directeur sportif, Johan Bruyneel, with the two of them allowing Ullrich's Telekom riders to take control of the race. Ultimately, though, it was revealed to be a stunning piece of bluffing followed by a real show of class on the final climb.

It's here, they say, where cycling traditionally reaches its summit. At 1,860 metres it's not all that high, but glory is there to be had at the end of the road to the top. It was up here that Fausto Coppi arrived in 1952, and since that moment the Alpe has become a sacred place to which the Tour keeps coming back as if paying homage to the saint of the road.

It's easy to understand why this ski station is viewed as the cathedral of climbs, especially when it is viewed from below. It's a most inspiring place to come to when the summer is upon us and the atmosphere is filled with the sound of tyres rushing by. Alpe d'Huez is a place of pilgrimage for cycling fans, the Versailles in their little kingdom. Each one of those fans climbing the 21 hairpins reawakens the echoes of shouts that have accompanied the idols, from Coppi onwards, who have climbed these slopes poker-faced and glistening with effort. They say faith releases a mountain of passion, and it's certainly true here.

The history of this enormous outcrop has achieved cult-like status. This mountain has given birth to a myth. Yesterday, the famous mountain did not betray that myth as cohorts of caravans stuck to its slopes that were packed with rows of multi-coloured sentinels. And still it is the orange hordes that dominate, all those boisterous Dutchmen and women who have laid siege to the citadel since the day when Coppi chewed up one of their own, a certain Nolten. By an ironic twist, they have made it their favourite mountain despite coming from the flattest of countries, a place where climbing onto a bar stool will provide you with a view of the sea. But in the end it was an American who produced one hell of a performance.

Since Hannibal's elephants first opened a path across the area, there has been nothing as crushing as this man Armstrong in these mountains. What was more head-turning in its shockingness was that this rider carried out such a feat in less time than it took to write about it or even to consider it. The famous Olympian imprecation of "higher, faster, stronger" was totally exemplified by an American who is undoubtedly stronger than the rest.

There was no doubt about Armstrong's mission on July 17, 2001. "Today I told the team that I wanted to win this stage because it is mythical. When I saw the Telekom team riding I was happy to follow without stirring myself too much. Then I gave it everything on the final climb. But I hope I don't pay for that effort in the time trial." And then Armstrong added: "I couldn't go any faster at the end. I think I attacked a bit too early. I'll be very tired this evening." Even an extraterrestrial can have its weaknesses!

CHRISTIAN MONTAIGNAC
L'EQUIPE, JULY 18, 2001

THE EAGLE TAKES OFF. Armstrong won't take the yellow jersey at the summit of Alpe d'Huez, but he is crushing the life out of his most likely challengers.

A champion the like of which we've never seen – or have we?

Lance Armstrong is an atypical champion. His style is described as unique, but in fact harks back to former times.

ARMSTRONG IS AN ATYPICAL champion because illness has changed his body and his style of riding; he is an atypical champion because his pedalling style is not at all the same as his contemporaries. But rate of pedalling (85-90 revolutions a minute yesterday on the climb of the Alpe) was once typical of his illustrious predecessors such as Bahamontes, Van Impe and other specialist climbers. And the recent revelation of his collaboration with the controversial Doctor Ferrari makes this all rather comical. Armstrong's pedalling style catches the eye because it stands out against that of his rivals, who have been educated with the sole aim of developing power and performance via the famous 'threshold' tests. In short, they have stuck to the doctrine laid down by the 'sports doctors', the sorcerers within the peloton, amongst whom Ferrari is the emblematic figure.

These people know all about the body and how to improve its function, but they've forgotten the words of Paul Koechli. What did the Swiss coach, who was Hinault's 'bike professor' late in his career, believe? That cycling is primarily an action, that this action is pedalling and that this task was the fundamental base of all success. Lance Armstrong may have read what Koechli said. In any case, even as a young rider he used to pedal like that, as was confirmed when his stage victory in 1993 was shown again.

So he has shown a certain degree of consistency. Yesterday Armstrong climbed the 14 kilometres to Alpe d'Huez 26 seconds slower than Pantani in 1997, which was a record for the hill. Checking his average speed against his pedalling ratio enables the conclusion to be drawn that he climbed most of the mountain in a very reasonable gear of 39x21. If the speed with which he established gaps over his principal rivals is added in, the large part of which he opened up on the lower slopes of the mountain, it can be concluded that he didn't go up more than a gear or two when the gradient lessened. So perhaps Armstrong does have a deficiency – a lack of power when searching for his second wind…

CLAUDE DROUSSENT
L'EQUIPE, JULY 18, 2001

Top left:
LAURENT ROUX was alone on his own from the col du Glandon where he dropped the Spaniard Jimenez. He will have more than six minutes in hand at the foot of the final climb to Alpe d'Huez…

Top right:
…BUT LANCE ARMSTRONG asked his team-mates to set the pace. He quickly goes on alone and swoops down on Roux six kilometres from the finish…

…THE TWO RIDERS are side by side: this is quite some picture because this situation only lasted a second at most. That's how long it took Armstrong to pass, without even a glance sideways, his unfortunate opponent.

L'ÉQUIPE,
July 18, 2001.

In the eagle's nest

Lance Armstrong also dominated everyone in his hotel. He was the victor in the midst of the vanquished.

HIS ARRIVAL AT THE hotel was almost provocative: Lance Armstrong came into the foyer leaving the photographers behind him. Then he crossed the foyer at such a speed, after 209 kilometres of racing, that those present were left looking stunned. He shook hands as he went, like a politician in the midst of a campaign, then took the lift to the top floor. While the eagle Armstrong was already in his eyrie, some exhausted riders in the last gruppetto were only just making for their hotels after finishing.

Martial Gayant, the deputy directeur sportif at La Française des Jeux, was collecting the keys to his room. A few minutes before he had seen Armstrong cross the foyer like a missile. "He's a monster when it comes to his level of recuperation. I saw him at the Tour of Switzerland and wondered: 'Who can beat this guy?' I'm not surprised. He loves to batter his opponents in the Alps. Of course our riders are dumbstruck with admiration for him."

8.42 in the evening. Lance Armstrong comes into the restaurant. The eagle swoops down on the buffet. When it comes to dessert he asks his dietitian to say yeah or nay to the cakes on display. Together they decide on a piece of tart and a small slice of chocolate cake. A few morsels of sweetness before battle is recommenced.

CHRISTINE THOMAS
L'EQUIPE, JULY 18, 2001

UNDER THE ADMIRING GAZE of Jean-Claude Gayssot, the minister of transport, and Jean-Marie Leblanc, the director of the Tour de France, Lance Armstrong crosses the finish line, exhausted but happy. He has produced a performance worthy of the legends of the Tour de France.

TREK
Thomas Weisel Partners
UNITED STATES POSTAL SERVICE
LYONNAIS
AGF
sport
KAWA

ALL THE WINNERS

1952

F. **Coppi** (ITA, Bianchi)

"I told myself I wouldn't strike first – I waited for Robic to attack."

1976

J. **Zoetemelk** (HOL, Gan-Mercier)

"I responded to Van Impe's attack: I wasn't sure that we could go any further."

1977

H. **Kuiper** (HOL, Ti-Raleigh)

"I felt very good. Full of energy – right at the top of my form."

ALL THE YELLOW JERSEYS

F. **Coppi** (ITA, Bianchi)

Coppi took on the yellow jersey that had been worn that day by his team-mate Carréa.

L. **Van Impe** (BEL, Gitane)

"I decided to break today because I felt like there was some business to be taken care of."

B. **Thévenet** (FRA, Peugeot)

"I had two blokes in tow – Kuiper et Van Impe – who both wanted to beat me."

1978

Two versions of the result – the first after Pollentier's win, and the second after his subsequent disqualification.

1979

There are two stages which finished at the Alpe in 1979 : Les Menuires– L'Alpe d'Huez (1) and L'Alpe d'Huez–L'Alpe d'Huez (2), the next day.

M. **Pollentier** (1)
(BEL, Velda-Lano Flandria)

"I had the chance today, because the wind in the valley was favourable."

H. **Kuiper** (2)
(HOL, Ti-Raleigh)

"It doesn't make me happy to win a stage like this."

J. **Agostinho** (1)
(POR, Sunair-Ca Va Seul-Flandria)

"I'm 36, so it's amazing to win such a big stage."

J. **Zoetemelk** (2)
(HOL, Miko-Mercier)

"Taking a few seconds out of Hinault probably won't make any difference to the overall result."

M. **Pollentier** (1)
(BEL, Velda-Lano Flandria)

"Now, the Tour is between Zoetemelk, Hinault and me."

J. **Zoetemelk** (2)
(HOL, Miko-Mercier-Hutchinson)

"The rules are there – you have to stick to them. And if you break them, you get punished."

B. **Hinault** (1)
(FRA, Renault-Gitane)

"From here on in, I'm quite happy just to follow my only rival, Joop Zoetemelk."

B. **Hinault** (2)
(FRA, Renault-Gitane)

"Zoetemelk took his chance very well, but I was never worried."

1981

P. **Winnen** (HOL, Capri Sonne)

"I felt like the final climb took five years off my life."

B. **Hinault** (FRA, Gitane)

"Now I have only two rivals to keep my eye on: Van Impe and Alban."

1982

B. **Breu** (SUI, Cilo-Aufina)

"I've got the best team in the world – this was a team win."

B. **Hinault** (FRA, Renault-Elf-Gitane)

"It's up to my rivals to take the initiative – not me!"

1983

P. **Winnen** (HOL, Ti-Raleigh-Campagnolo)

"It's crazy that I won the stage – I felt bad all day."

L. **Fignon** (FRA, Renault-Elf-Gitane)

"Today, I feel capable of anything. They'll have to tear the yellow jersey off my back."

1984

L. **Herrera** (COL, Colombie-Varta)

"I was suffering badly at the start of the climb – Fignon seemed much stronger to me."

L. **Fignon** (FRA, Renault-Elf)

"I knew that I'd take the yellow jersey in the Alps – either here or somewhere else."

1986

B. **Hinault** (FRA, La Vie Claire)

"I'm proud of what happened with Greg – but the Tour's not over yet."

G. **LeMond** (USA, La Vie Claire)

Hinault: "I didn't offer the Tour to Greg LeMond – but to our team."

1987

F. **Echave** (SPA, BH)

"I attacked because I wanted to help Fuente on the stage."

P. **Delgado** (SPA, PDM)

"I was talking with Luis Ocaña yesterday – he predicted I'd get the yellow jersey today."

1988

S. **Rooks** (HOL, PDM)

"In Holland, they'll be calling this the sweetest win of my career."

P. **Delgado** (SPA, Reynolds)

"I owe everything to my team-mates. Without them, I wouldn't be in the yellow jersey."

1989

G-J. **Theunisse** (HOL, PDM)

"My rhythm got me through the last climb – it didn't hurt at all."

L. **Fignon** (FRA, Super U)

"I came up Alpe d'Huez on some kind of cloud – without any difficulties."

1990

G. **Bugno** (ITA, Château d'Ax)

"During the climb, I decided to think of nothing but winning the stage."

R. **Pensec** (FRA, Z)

"I've got the yellow jersey and my team-mate Greg LeMond is third. It's going well, isn't it?"

1991

G. **Bugno** (ITA, Château d'Ax)

"I tried to shake Indurain off, but I couldn't. He's too strong."

M. **Indurain** (SPA, Banesto)

"I was dreading this stage more than any other – I was happy to come in behind Bugno!"

1992

A. **Hampsten** (USA, Motorola)

"I've dreamed of winning this stage for as long as I can remember – it's a magical feeling."

M. **Indurain** (SPA, Banesto)

"I said that everything would be clearer after Alpe d'Huez."

1994

R. **Conti** (ITA, Lampre-Panaria)

"The true champions are the riders who know how to take risks."

M. **Indurain** (SPA, Banesto)

"Part of managing a race is knowing how to ride your luck."

1995

M. **Pantani** (ITA, Carrera)

"All the great riders have made their mark at Alpe d'Huez."

M. **Indurain** (SPA, Banesto)

"The race really started today – I really had to look to my team."

1997

M. **Pantani** (ITA, Mercatone Uno)

"This win was more to do with my mental will than my physical strength."

J. **Ullrich** (GER, Telekom)

In yellow since the Pyrenees, Ullrich was seemingly untouchable all the way to Paris.

1999

G. **Guerini** (ITA, Telekom)

"I was in pieces at the bottom of the climb – but I came back together again on the way up."

L. **Armstrong** (USA, US Postal)

Greg LeMond: "What Lance has done in the Tour de France is impressive."

2001

L. **Armstrong** (USA, US Postal)

"I played a game of poker with Telekom today – and I won."

F. **Simon** (FRA, Bonjour)

"In my beautiful yellow jersey, I'm afraid of doing something wrong."

1952 – 10th stage
Lausanne –Alpe d'Huez (266km)

I. COPPI (ITA)
266km in 8-51-40
(average: 30.018km/h).
2. Robic (FRA) at 1-20
3. Ockers (BEL) at 3-22.
4. Gelabert (SPA).
5. Dotto (FRA) at 3-27
6. Carrea (ITA) at 3-29.
7. P. Molineris (FRA) at 4-00
8. Nolten (HOL) at 4-02
9. F. Magni (ITA) at 4-13
10. Close (BEL) at 4-15

OVERALL
I. **Coppi (ITA) 62-52-15**
2. **Carrea (ITA), at 0-05**
3. **Magni (ITA), at 1-56**
4. **Lauredi (FRA), at 5-01**
5. **Close (BEL), at 7-06**

1976 – 9th stage
Divonne les Bains -Alpe d'Huez (258km)

I. ZOETEMELK (HOL),
258km in 8-31-49
(average: 30.304km/h).
2. Van Impe (BEL) at 0-03.
3. Galdos (SPA) at 0-58
4. Romero (FRA) at 1-38
5. F. Bertoglio (ITA) at 1-45
6. Gi. Baronchelli (ITA)
7. R. Martin (FRA) at 1-50
8. Thévenet (FRA)
9. Poulidor (FRA)
10. Riccomi (ITA) at 2-00

OVERALL
I. **Van Impe (BEL)**
49-27-32
2. **Zoetemelk (HOL) at 0-08**
3. **Maertens (BEL) at 54**
4. **Poulidor (FRA) at 1-24**
5. **Baronchelli (ITA) at 1-39**

1977-17th stage
Chamonix Mont Blanc -L Alpe-d'Huez
(184.5km)

I. KUIPER (HOL)
184.5km in 6-00-20
(average: 30.721km/h).
2. Thévenet (FRA) at 0-41
3. Van Impe (BEL) at 2-06
4. Galdos (SPA) at 2-59
5. Zoetemelk (HOL) at 4-40
6. R. Martin (FRA) at 8-15
7. Pozo (SPA) at 8-39
8. Agostinho (POR) at 8-44
9. Laurent (FRA) at 9-29
10. P. Torres (SPA) at 10-49

OVERALL
I. **Thévenet (FRA)**
97-35-51
2. **Kuiper (HOL) at 0-08**
3. **Van Impe (BEL) at 1-58**
4. **Galdos (SPA) at 4-14**
5. **Zoetemelk (HOL) at 5-12**

1978 – 16th stage
Saint Étienne -Alpe d'Huez (240.5km)

I. KUIPER (HOL)
240.5km in 7-23-45
(average: 31.820km/h)
2. Hinault (FRA) at 0-08
3. Zoetemelk (HOL) at 0-41
4. Agostinho (POR) at 1-34
5. Lubberding (HOL)
     at 2-14
6. Van Impe (BEL) at 2-23
7. Galdos (SPA)
8. Nilsson (SWE) at 3-25
9. P. Wellens (BEL) at 3-43
10. R. Martin (FRA) at 4-48

OVERALL
I. **Zoetemelk (HOL)**
80-6-41
2. **Hinault (FRA) at 0-14**
3. **Kuiper (HOL) at 5-31**
4. **Agostinho (POR)**
at 6-10
5. **J. Bruyère (BEL)**
at 9-32

1979 – 17th stage
Les Menuires-Alpe d'Huez (166.5km)

I. AGOSTINHO (POR)
166.5km in 6-12-55
(average: 27.272km/h).
2. Alban (FRA) at 1-57
3. P. Wellens (BEL) at 2-45
4. M. Laurent (FRA) at 2-48
5. Bernaudeau (FRA) at 3-17
6. Nilsson (SWE) at 3-19
7. Battaglin (ITA)
8. Hinault (FRA)
9. Zoetemelk (HOL)
10. R. Martin (FRA) at 3-34

OVERALL
I. **Hinault (FRA)**
69-38-15
2. **Zoetemelk (HOL) at 2-45**
3. **Kuiper (HOL) at 19-22**
4. **Bernaudeau (FRA)**
at 20-58
5. **Agostinho (POR)**
at 21-40

1979 – 18th stage
Alpe d'Huez-Alpe d'Huez (118.5km)

I. ZOETEMELK (HOL)
118.5km in 4-23-28
(average: 26.986km/h).
2. Van Impe (BEL) at 0-40
3. Hinault (FRA) at 0-47
4. Agostinho (POR) at 1-05
5. Battaglin (ITA) at 2-21
6. E. Martinez (SPA)
7. P. Wellens (BEL) at 2-23
8. Kuiper (HOL) at 2-48
9. Bernaudeau (FRA) at 3-29
10. Levavasseur (FRA)

OVERALL
I. **Hinault (FRA)**
74-02-30
2. **Zoetemelk (HOL) at 1-58**
3. **Kuiper (HOL) at 21-23**
4. **Agostinho (POR)**
at 21-58
5. **Bernaudeau (FRA)**
at 23-40

1981 – 19th stage
Morzine -Alpe d'Huez (230.5km)

I. WINNEN (HOL)
230.5km in 7-36-18
(average: 30.506km/h).
2. Hinault (FRA) at 0-08
3. Van Impe (BEL) at 0-09
4. Alban (FRA) at 0-12
5. J. De Muynck (BEL) at 1-38
6. Zoetemelk (HOL) at 2-01
7. Criquielion (BEL) at 3-23
8. P. Wellens (BEL) at 3-33
9. A. De Wolf (BEL) at 4-14
10. Bernaudeau (FRA) at 4-16

OVERALL
I. **Hinault (FRA) 77-32-27**
2. **Van Impe (BEL) at 9-39**
3. **Alban (FRA) at 10-49**
4. **Zoetemelk (HOL)**
at 12-36
5. **J. De Muynck (BEL)**
at 12-58

1982 – 16th stage
Orcières -Alpe d'Huez (123km)

I. BREU (SWI)
123km in 3-24-22
(average: 36.112km/h).
2. Alban (FRA) at 0-16
3. A. Fernandez (SPA)
     at 1-18
4. R. Martin (FRA) at 1-22
5. Hinault (FRA) at 1-26
6. Zoetemelk (HOL)
7. Winnen (HOL)
8. Vallet (FRA) at 2-12
9. Van de Velde (HOL)
10. P. Wellens (BEL) at 2-51

OVERALL
I. **Hinault (FRA)**
67-19-28
2. **Zoetemelk (HOL)**
at 5-26
3. **Breu (SWI) at 9-16**
4. **Winnen (HOL) at 9-40**
5. **Vallet (FRA) at 10-50**

1983 – 17th stage
La Tour du Pin-Alpe d'Huez (223km)

I. WINNEN (HOL)
223km in 7-21-32
(average: 30.303km/h).
2. Bernaudeau (FRA)
3. Corredor (COL) at 0-57
4. Alban (FRA) at 1-22
5. Fignon (FRA) at 2-07
6. Van Impe (BEL) at 2-08
7. Delgado (SPA) at 2-10
8. R. Martin (FRA) at 2-42
9. Jimenez (COL) at 3-05
10. Veldscholten (HOL)
     at 3-07

OVERALL
I. **Fignon (FRA)**
82-27-28
2. **Delgado (SPA) at 1-08**
3. **Bernaudeau (FRA)**
at 2-33
4. **Winnen (HOL) at 3-31**
5. **Kelly (IRL) at 4-20**

1984 – 17th stage
Grenoble -Alpe d'Huez (151km)

I. HERRERA (COL)
151km in 4-39-24
(average: 32.426km/h).
2. Fignon (FRA) at 0-49
3. Arroyo (SPA) at 2-27
4. Millar (GBR) at 3-05
5. Acevedo (FRA) at 3-09
6. LeMond (USA) at 3-30
7. Hinault (FRA) at 3-44
8. P. Simon (FRA) at 3-58
9. Wilches (COL) at 4-10
10. Munoz (SPA) at 4-12

OVERALL
I. **Fignon (FRA)**
79-24-56
2. **Barteau (FRA) at 4-22**
3. **Hinault (FRA) at 5-41**
4. **Millar (GBR) at 8-25**
5. **LeMond (USA) at 8-45**

1986 – 18th stage
Briançon-Alpe d'Huez (162.5km)

1. **HINAULT,**
162.5km in 5-03-03
(average: 32.172km/h).
2. LeMond (USA)
3. Zimmermann (SWI)
at 5-15
4. Montoya (COL) at 6-06
5. Y. Madiot (FRA) at 6-21
6. Hampsten (USA) at 6-22
7. Pensec (FRA) at 6-26
8. S. Cabrera (COL) at 6-34
9. P. Simon (FRA) at 6-45
10. A. Pino (SPA) at 6-48

OVERALL
1. **LeMond (USA)**
at 86-27-13
2. **Hinault (FRA) at 2-45**
3. **Zimmermann (SWI)**
at 7-41
4. **Hampsten (USA)**
at 16-48
5. **Pensec (FRA) at 21-34**

1987 – 20th stage
Villard de Lans-Alpe d'Huez (201km)

1. **ECHAVE (SPA)**
201km in 5-52-11
(average: 34.243km/h).
2. Fuerte (SPA) at 1-32
3. Lavainne (FRA) at 2-12
4. M. Ramirez (COL) at 3-00
5. Herrera (COL) at 3-19
6. Fignon (FRA) at 3-25
7. Delgado (SPA) at 3-44
8. Van Calster (BEL) at 3-44
9. Criquielion (BEL) at 4-23
10. Zadrobilek (AUT) at 4-43

OVERALL
1. **Delgado (SPA)**
90-32-20
2. **Roche (IRL) at 0-25**
3. **Bernard (FRA) at 2-02**
4. **Mottet (FRA) at 2-12**
5. **Herrera (COL) at 5-03**

1988 – 12th stage
Morzine-Alpe d'Huez (227km)

1. **ROOKS (HOL)**
227km in 6-55-44
(average: 32.76km/h).
2. Theunisse (HOL) at 0-17
3. Delgado (SPA)
4. Parra (COL) at 0-23
5. Herrera (COL) at 1-06
6. Claveyrolat (FRA) at 2-31
7. Bauer (CAN) at 2-34
8. Boyer (FRA) at 3-08
9. Winnen (HOL)
10. Hampsten (USA) at 4-21

OVERALL
1. **Delgado (SPA)**
47-03-13
2. **Bauer (CAN) at 0-25**
3. **Parra (COL) at 1-20**
4. **Rooks (HOL) at 1-38**
5. **Herrera (COL) at 2-25**

1989 – 12th stage
Briançon-Alpe d'Huez (165km)

1. **THEUNISSE (HOL)**
165km in 5-10-39
(average: 31.868km/h).
2. Delgado (SPA) at 1-09
3. Fignon (FRA) .
4. Rondon (COL) at 2-08
5. LeMond (USA) at 2-28
6. Lejarreta (SPA) at 2-41
7. Rooks (HOL) at 3-04
8. Bugno (ITA) m.t.
9. Millar (GBR) at 3-08
10. P. Simon (FRA) at 3-48

OVERALL
1. **Fignon (FRA)**
77-55-11
2. **LeMond (USA) at 0-26**
3. **Delgado (SPA)**
at 1-55
4. **Theunisse (HOL) at 5-12**
5. **Mottet (FRA) at 5-22**

THE HÔTELIER GEORGES RAJON (top right, in the company of his wife), one of the innovators of this great event, welcomes 1968 Tour winner Jan Janssen (centre) and his team-mates.

1990 – 11th stage
Saint Gervais - Alpe d'Huez (182.5km)

1. **BUGNO (ITA)**
182.5km in 5-37-51
(average: 32.410km/h).
2. LeMond (USA)
3. Breukink (HOL) at 0-01
4. Claveyrolat (FRA) at 0-04
5. Parra (COL) at 0-06
6. Rondon (COL) at 0-40
7. Hampsten (USA)
8. Delgado (SPA)
9. Criquielion (BEL) at 0-47
10. Pensec (FRA) at 0-48

OVERALL
1. **Pensec (FRA)**
48-24-43
2. **Chiappucci (ITA) at 1-28**
3. **LeMond (USA) at 9-04**
4. **Breukink (HOL) at 9-28**
5. **Bugno (ITA) at 10-39**

1991 – 17th stage
Gap -Alpe d'Huez (125km)

1. **BUGNO (ITA)**
125km in 3-25-48
(average: 36.443km/h).
2. Indurain (SPA) at 0-01
3. Leblanc (FRA) at 0-02
4. Bernard (FRA) at 0-35
5. Rooks (HOL) at 0-43
6. Chiappucci (ITA)
7. Claveyrolat (FRA)
8. Delgado (SPA) at 0-45
9. Fignon (FRA) at 1-12
10. Mejia (COL) at 1-13

OVERALL
1. **Indurain (SPA)**
79-05-25
2. **Bugno (ITA) at 3-09**
3. **Chiappucci (ITA)**
at 4-48
4. **Mottet (FRA) at 4-57**
5. **LeMond (USA) at 6-39**

1992 – 14th stage
Sestrières-Alpe d'Huez (186,5km)

1. **HAMPSTEN (USA)**
186.5km in 5-41-58
(average: 36.785km/h).
2. Vona (ITA) at 1-17
3. Boyer (FRA) at 2-08
4. Nevens (BEL) at 2-46
5. Chiappucci (ITA) at 3-15
6. Indurain (SPA) at 3-15
7. Unzaga (SPA) at 3-28
8. Virenque (FRA) 4-04
9. Theunisse (HOL) at 4-13
10. Breukink (HOL) at 4-42

OVERALL
1. **Indurain (SPA)**
69-20-07
2. **Chiappucci (ITA) at 1-42**
3. **Hampsten (USA) at 8-01**
4. **Lino (FRA) at 9-16**
5. **Bugno (ITA) at 10-09**

1994 – 16th stage
Valréas-Alpe d'Huez (224.5km)

1. **CONTI (ITA)**
224.5km in 6-06-45
(average: 32.014km/h).
2. Buenahora (COL) at 2-02
3. Bolts (ALL) at 3-49
4. Elli (ITA)
5. Perini (ITA) at 4-03
6. Muller (SWI) at 4-39
7. Cenghialta (ITA) at 5-05
8. Pantani (ITA) at 5-41
9. Torres (SPA) at 5-55
10. Camargo (COL) at 7-15

OVERALL
1. **Indurain (SPA)**
81-26-16
2. **Virenque (FRA) at 7-21**
3. **Leblanc (FRA) at 8-35**
4. **De las Cuevas (FRA)**
at 9-15
5. **Pantani (ITA) at 9-40**

1995 – 10th stage
Aime La Plagne -Alpe d'Huez (162.5km)

1. **PANTANI (ITA)**
162.5km in 5-13-14
(average: 31.127km/h).
2. Indurain (SPA) at 1-24
3. Zulle (SWI) .
4. Riis (DEN) at 1-26
5. Madouas (FRA) at 1-54
6. Escartin (SPA) at 2-01
7. Jalabert (FRA) at 2-26
8. Virenque (FRA) at 2-50
9. Gotti (ITA)
10. Chiappucci (ITA) at 3-02

OVERALL
1. **Indurain (SPA)**
42-32-58
2. **Zulle (SWI) at 2-27**
3. **Riis (DEN) at 6-00**
4. **Rominger (SWI) at 8-19**
5. **Gotti (ITA) at 8-20**

1997 – 13th stage
Saint Étienne-Alpe d'Huez (203.5km)

1. **PANTANI (ITA)**
203.5km in 5-02-42
(average: 40.3km/h).
2. Ullrich (GER) at 0-47
3. Virenque (FRA) at 1-27
4. Casagrande (ITA) at 2-27
5. Riis (DEN) at 2-28
6. Zberg (SWI) at 2-59
7. Bolts (GER)
8. Conti (ITA)
9. Madouas (FRA)
10. Jalabert (FRA) at 3-22

OVERALL
1. **Ullrich (GER) 7-00-26**
2. **Virenque (FRA) at 6-22**
3. **Riis (DEN) at 11-06**
4. **Pantani (ITA) at 11-39**
5. **Olano (SPA) at 14-28**

1999 – 10th stage
Sestrières-Alpe d'Huez (220.5km).

1. **GUERINI (ITA)**
220.5km in 6-42-31
(average: 32.868km/h).
2. Tonkov (RUS) at 0-21
3. Escartin (SPA) at 0-25
4. Zulle (SWI)
5. Armstrong (USA)
6. Virenque (FRA)
7. Dufaux (SWI)
8. Van de Wouwer (BEL)
9. Beltran (SPA) at 0-32
10. Contreras (COL) at 0-49

OVERALL
1. **Armstrong (USA)**
46-14-03
2. **Olano (SPA) at 7-42**
3. **Zulle (SWI) at 7-47**
4. **Dufaux (SWI) at 8-07**
5. **Escartin (SPA) at 8-53**

2001 – 10th stage
Aix les Bains -Alpe d'Huez (209km)

1. **ARMSTRONG (USA)**
209km in 6-23-47
(average: 32.675km/h).
2. Ullrich (GER) at 1-59
3. Beloki (SPA) at 2-09
4. Moreau (FRA) at 2-30
5. Sevilla (SPA) at 2-54
6. Mancebo (SPA) at 4-01
7. Roux (FRA) at 4-03
8. I. Gonzalez de Galdeano (SPA)
9. Laiseka (SPA)
10. Piepoli (ITA) at 4-07

OVERALL
1. **Simon (FRA) 45-34-09**
2. **Kivilev (KAZ) at 11-54**
3. **O'Grady (AUS) at 18-10**
4. **Armstrong (USA)**
at 20-07
5. **Beloki (SPA) at 21-42**